HOW TO
BUY A FLAT

HOW TO
BUY A FLAT

All you need to
know about
apartment
living and
letting

Liz Hodgkinson

howtobooks

DEDICATION
for my wonderful goddaughter Georgia

Published by How To Books Ltd
3 Newtec Place, Magdalen Road
Oxford OX4 1RE, United Kingdom
Tel: (01865) 793806. Fax: (01865) 248780
email: info@howtobooks.co.uk
www.howtobooks.co.uk

British Library Cataloguing in Publication Data
A catalogue record for this book is available from the British Library

Cover design by Baseline Arts Ltd, Oxford
Produced for How To Books by Deer Park Productions, Tavistock, Devon
Typeset by PDQ Typesetting, Newcastle-under-Lyme, Staffs.
Printed and bound by Cromwell Press, Trowbridge, Wiltshire

NOTE: The material contained in this book is set out in good faith for general guidance and no liability can be accepted for loss or expense incurred as a result of relying in particular circumstances on statements made in the book. The laws and regulations are complex and liable to change, and readers should check the current position with the relevant authorities before making personal arrangements.

Contents

Preface

Before long, there will be more people living in flats or apartments than houses. All over the world, more apartment blocks than separate houses are being built, even in countries which still have plenty of building land left.

This means that in future, large numbers of people are going to have to take on board a completely different way of living and relating to neighbours.

When you live in a flat, you may have people above and below you as well as next door and along the corridor. With flats, everybody is interconnected in a way that does not happen with even the most closely-packed terraced houses, and because of this there have to be strict rules to ensure that all residents behave in a responsible and community-minded fashion.

Not only that, but *buying* a flat is a completely different process from buying a house.

When you buy a house, you purchase the freehold and that is that. To all intents and purposes, you own the land on which your house stands until the end of time, or until you come to sell. This applies even with terraced or semi-detached houses.

Flats, though, are usually sold leasehold, which means in effect that you buy a length of tenure, rather than the actual property.

Your flat may be sold with a specific length of lease remaining. Or, it may be sold with a share of the freehold. Or, it may be sold 'commonhold'. There may be several layers of ownership, such as 'head leaseholder' or 'under-leaseholder'. There may be managing agents, residents' committees and a Board of Directors, none of which apply when you buy a house.

Then, when you buy a flat, shelling out money does not end with the purchase. You have to continue to pay monthly service charges, to ensure the building remains in good repair. And you must legally abide by the terms of the lease you have signed before completion.

What does it all mean? What are your rights, and what are your responsibilities when you buy a flat? This book explains all, and tells how to get the very best out of this modern and increasingly common way of living.

Flats can be safer, warmer, cleaner, easier and cheaper to run and also friendlier than houses. They are ideal for single people, young couples, busy workers, older people downsizing or, in fact, anybody who does not want the fuss and bother of looking after an entire house. Apartments are often in vastly better and more central locations than houses, and there is a huge choice of styles available.

The vast majority of property investors buy flats, rather than houses, to let out. But before buying a flat, either to live in yourself, or rent out, you need to know exactly what you are letting yourself in for.

Liz Hodgkinson

Introduction

Nowadays, ever more people are living in flats rather than whole houses. At one time, flat living was relatively rare but in England and Wales at least, more flats than houses have been built since 2003, and over 100,000 new flats are now being built each year.

In April 2000, just 16.5 per cent of properties bought in Britain were flats, but by March 2005, this figure had risen to 20.5 per cent. Over 72 per cent of all properties bought in London are now flats, and in 2004, 40 per cent of all homes built by Barratt, Britain's biggest housebuilder, were flats. This is more than twice as many as ten years previously.

Worldwide, the vast majority of newbuild properties are apartment blocks rather than houses, and as the population inexorably expands and becomes ever more urban, it seems that separate houses will one day be the rarer type of dwelling.

But the ever-increasing popularity of flat living is not only to do with population growth and housing demand.

CHEAPER FOR DEVELOPERS

One significant aspect is that, so far as developers and builders are concerned, it is cheaper and easier to build blocks of flats rather than individual houses.

Where land is scarce but demand is high, as in waterfront locations and inner cities, for instance, it may no longer be possible to build separate houses for everybody. Also, even where there is space, it is easier to obtain planning permission for apartment blocks which will house many people, than for a few detached five-bedroom houses standing in their own landscaped gardens. As you can build more dwellings on less land, acquiring land is cheaper, too. Then there is great encouragement to build on brownfield sites – where there has already been a building of some kind – rather than on greenfield sites.

It is most common for apartment blocks to be built on brownfield sites; greenfield sites are usually reserved for separate houses, but it is much more difficult to get planning permission to build on these sites than where it is already built up.

Apartments can be squeezed in where it would be impossible to put a house, such as on top of supermarkets, for instance, and all kinds of previously non-residential premises such as fire stations, warehouses, libraries, schools, factories and police stations can quite easily be converted, and are being converted – into apartment buildings. For example, The Old Fire Station, the Old Brewery, the Old Candle Factory are becoming very smart addresses.

It is also easier and cheaper to lay on services such as electricity, gas and water to an apartment block than to a series of separate houses. Architects like the challenge of apartment blocks because they can go to town, whereas they are severely restricted to thinking 'inside the box' with separate houses.

ALTERING DEMOGRAPHICS

There was once a distinct stigma about living in a flat rather than a house but this is fast disappearing and cost and density are not the only reasons for this. Ever more people are now living on their own, and young singles and couples, divorced and separated people and the elderly, increasingly do not want to live in a whole house but prefer the ease and security of a flat. Most retirement and 'age-exclusive' housing, for instance, consists of apartments rather than houses, and for the majority of first-time buyers, their starter home is now a flat, not a house.

ADVANTAGES OF FLAT LIVING

Nowadays, flats afford more lifestyle and location options than houses, and depending on pocket and preference, you can go for a tiny studio in a very central location, or have a huge rambling flat in an imposing Edwardian mansion block.

You can go for a characterful Victorian conversion or an ultra-modern apartment in an award-winning new building.

Flats tend to be more secure than houses and the modern ones at least, have far more amenities. It might be difficult to afford your own private gym or swimming pool with a house, but spas and fitness centres are increasingly a factor of even quite modest blocks of flats.

Plus, with a flat, you can have the modern equivalent of servants or staff, such as porters, gardeners, valet parking, painters and decorators and cleaners. And the more people there are to share each amenity, the cheaper it becomes.

When you buy a flat, you can have a much more luxurious style of living than you would be able to afford with a house. You can also enjoy stupendous views on the top storeys of an apartment building; views which would be inaccessible with even the tallest house.

If you are away a lot or like to travel, you can lock up and leave a flat in a way that would be extremely difficult with a house.

Because so much of the building is shared, it is usually cheaper to live in a flat than a house. Utility bills are vastly cheaper, and as all works and exterior decoration are shared between the residents, renovation and upkeep costs less.

Also, size for size, flats feel more spacious than houses. A house of 2,500 square feet can feel tight, as corridors, stairwells, halls and landings have to be squeezed into this footage, whereas a flat of the same size can feel extremely spacious.

DISDAVANTAGES TO FLAT LIVING

The overwhelming drawback to buying a flat is that the property will almost always be sold leasehold rather than freehold which means, in effect, that you are buying a length of tenure rather than the property outright. By contrast, when you buy a house, you buy the freehold, which means you own the property in perpetuity.

Apart from the extremely complex laws concerning the tenure of apartment blocks, there is also the fact that you may have up to 200 near neighbours to contend with, all living on top of each other.

UNDERSTANDING LEASEHOLD LAW

Many laws relating to the tenure of apartments are difficult to understand and even conveyancing solicitors often do not fully appreciate all their complexities and subtleties. Nor do mortgage lenders, it must be said.

Although you enjoy many ownership rights with a long lease which does not happen when you rent month by month, as the lease runs down, your flat will be worth ever less, and by the time the term is up, your stake is worth nothing. At this time, it will automatically revert to the freeholder, or landlord. You often see examples of the rundown lease in very upmarket London postcodes, where 16-year leases are frequently offered for sale in places like Eaton Square. Often, such leases cost around £500,000 – about the price it would cost to rent that property for a similar length of time.

The lease itself is a lengthy, legally-binding document written in offputtingly archaic and tortuous legalese. Many leaseholders have never even glanced at the lease before buying and have no idea of its terms. Then they are later appalled if they are accused of breaching one of its hundreds of clauses and schedules.

Strictly speaking, a leaseholder is known as a tenant, and somebody who rents from the leaseholder is referred to as a sub-tenant. The actual owner of the property is the freeholder, or landlord, and this means the person who owns the actual building and ultimately, the units within it.

Leasehold law comes somewhere between owning and renting and is in many ways a horrible hybrid which governments have been trying to simplify for decades, even now without complete success. In fact, some legal experts claim that every time the government attempts to simplify leasehold laws, it ends up making them even more complicated.

Summary
To sum up, when you buy a flat, you buy a length of lease rather than outright ownership. New leases tend to be either 99 years or 125 years long, but can be 999 years. Although you can sell this lease on to another buyer, the shorter the lease gets, the less valuable the property becomes. So, a lease is a wasting asset.

Leases can also in extreme cases be forfeited, for persistent and wilful breaching of the clauses. Where this happens, the leaseholder loses everything, even when there are many years left on the lease.

LEASEHOLD WITH A SHARE OF THE FREEHOLD
To make matters even more complicated, some flats are sold leasehold with a share of the freehold. This means there is no outside freeholder or landlord, and the residents collectively own the building. In other words, the lunatics are running the asylum or, to put it more kindly, the shareholders own the company, and can set their own agenda.

But even if there is an outside freeholder, all is not lost as it is now possible to enfranchise, which means the leaseholders can get together to buy the freehold from the landlord, and so take control. It is also legally possible in many cases to extend short leases by 90 years, at a price, of course.

Leaseholders subject to an outside freeholder can also exercise Right to Manage, which is another way of taking control. Leasehold flats are becoming an ever more secure way to own a home, but there are still many anomalies. Because leasehold law is so very complex, there are now firms of lawyers and experts specialising entirely in this aspect.

COMMONHOLD

Since 2004, when the Commonhold and Leasehold Reform Act of 2002 was implemented it has also been theoretically possible to buy flats with a new type of tenure known as Commonhold. Here, there is no outside freeholder, and the commonholders collectively own the common parts as well as their own individual units. But the new commonhold, as will be explained later, is just as complicated as the old leasehold.

Other problems

There are very many laws and regulations relating to apartment living, not just because of the ramifications of leasehold and commonhold laws, but also because ways have to be found of ensuring that residents living cheek by jowl and sharing many common areas, are enabled to exist in reasonable harmony with each other.

A NATURAL WAY OF LIVING?

Although living in a flat makes such a lot of sense these days from so many points of view, the real problems arise not so much because of leasehold/freehold issues, important though they are, but because it is basically unnatural for humans, and indeed, most species, to live on top of one another.

Apart from some insects like ants and honeybees, most creatures have their own individual dens, lairs or nests. Even when masses of birds congregate on a cliff, you will notice that each keeps to its own space, however small. Humans are no different. Notice how all passengers try to maintain their own space in a crowded tube train, for instance, and pretend that the traveller jammed up tight against them is not really there at all. There is a deep instinct to be territorial, to mark out your own space and with flat living, you cannot really do this. True, you will have your own lockable front door, but it will most likely be on a shared corridor. And, as with a hotel room, you will usually have people above and below and be able to hear their footsteps and comings and goings.

This is why, in the past, great lords and aristocrats built their own massive homes well away from prying eyes. The richer you were, the more you could afford to indulge this basic instinct for privacy. It was only the desperately poor people who had to live on top of each other, in tenements and rookeries or attics and garrets. In the past, success in life meant having your very own house and, until very recently, this remained the aspiration of most people.

It is still true that rich and successful people buy large detached houses in their own grounds but it is also true that these same rich and successful people will often own a modern flat in a centrally-located apartment, so as to have the best of both worlds. One only has to think of Jeffrey Archer, with his main home, the Old Vicarage, Grantchester and London penthouse flat overlooking the river.

But however lavishly appointed your flat is, you cannot get away from the fact that you will be sharing a roof, foundations, common parts and common amenities, with a load of strangers. When individual flats change hands, you have no control over who buys the flat next door to you, or above or below you.

THE NATURE OF INTERCONNECTION

Flat living means that the fabric of your home will be connected to other people's homes in a way that does not happen with even the most closely packed terraced houses.

You will share pipework, for instance, and you will share external walls, drains and guttering. You will probably share a lift and a main front door and although each flat dweller will have a separate electricity, gas and water meter, the supply will come from a common source. You will most likely share a common television aerial. If a neighbour leaves a tap running on the top floor, this will eventually flood the basement. If renovations are being carried on in one flat, the whole building may be affected.

When major works are being carried out to one part of the building, this often means scaffolding will go past your windows, blocking out your light.

Because of this close interconnection, there are strict rules on what each owner is allowed to do. Unlike living in a separate house, compromises have to be made. You may not be allowed to hang washing out of the window, to vacuum the place or use the washing machine at certain hours; you will not be allowed to put rubbish in the corridors or leave bikes or prams in the hall – all of which you could do if you so wished in your own home.

You may not be allowed a satellite dish, and in some very upmarket blocks, you may not even be allowed to choose your own type of curtains. You will certainly not be allowed to choose your own type of window, as with apartment buildings a uniform look is always desired.

So, a level of conformity is essential if flat living is to work.

RUNNING THE BUILDING

Unlike a separate house, a block of flats has to be run, and run by somebody, adding further to the complications.

Where there is an outside freeholder, there will usually be managing agents appointed by that freeholder. Managing agents do not own the block and are simply employees of the freeholder or landlord. But they are given powers to run the building and it is their duty to make sure service charges are collected, that quotations are obtained for major works, and for ensuring that the terms of the lease are met by every occupant.

Even when the block is very small, as with a house divided into two flats, somebody still has to be responsible for insurance, exterior works and general maintenance.

COSTS CAN GO ON ...

Because common and exterior parts have to be constantly maintained in an apartment building, for the good of all, you have not finished shelling out when you buy a flat. Every month or every quarter, you are required to pay service charges for cleaning, porterage, rubbish clearance, exterior decoration, gardening and also any services which are, or may be, used by all residents, such as the lift.

These charges can vary from a few hundred pounds each year in a small, easily-maintained block, to £10,000 or more in a luxury block. It is your duty as a leaseholder to pay these charges, whether or not you agree with the amount.

There may also be extra levies raised from time to time, to pay for major works such as a new roof, which are not covered by ordinary charges.

There are now ways that excessive charges to leaseholders can be challenged, in tribunals and courts, but if they are deemed to be 'reasonable' you have a legal duty to pay them. If nobody pays service charges, the block may become dilapidated and decrease in value, so everybody eventually loses out.

So it is very much up to every occupant to pull their weight, to maintain the integrity and value of the building and each individual unit within it.

THE PROS AND CONS OF LIVING IN A FLAT

Here are the main pros and cons of living in a flat.

Pros

- You have neighbours who can look out for you.
- You may well have a porter who can also look out for you.
- Living in a flat is cheaper than living in a house.
- Utility bills are lower in a flat.
- Flats tend to be more secure than houses.
- There is a greater choice of location and size with a flat.
- Flats are friendlier than houses and tend to be nearer to shops, transport links and restaurants and bars.

- There is less risk of burglary in a flat.
- Leasehold law, although complex, is much fairer than it used to be and there is now almost as much security of tenure with a flat as with a house.

Cons

- You are never the outright owner.
- You have to be prepared for communal living.
- You cannot maintain the block on your own as this depends on a group effort.
- Flats can be noisy.
- You are more intimately connected with your neighbours than in a house.
- It is not always easy to soundproof flats.
- Neighbour disputes are common.
- You are dependent on everybody paying their way.
- You inevitably have less control over your environment than in a house.
- Factions and splinter groups can form.
- You have to make compromises.
- The value of a flat may not rise as much as with a house.

CASE STUDIES

I have found that when flat living works, it works wonderfully well. Although at times it can feel like being in the midst of a large dysfunctional family where warring factions abound, when everybody pulls together, there can be a lot of friendliness and fun when living in a flat.

For most of my life I have lived in a house but just recently I sold my house and bought two flats instead as my homes. This means I have a seafront home and a central London home, either of which can be easily locked up and left. Also, I can constantly escape if one or the other gets too much! If I feel like a few days in London, I can just lock up my seafront flat and head off – and vice versa.

Because I am always meeting my neighbours in the corridor, lift or at the front door, I have formed friendships that could not have happened as a houseowner. My flats are manageable, easy to keep clean and relatively cheap to run. There is no way I could afford two houses in similar locations, so I have choice and freedom by living in the flats instead.

Also, now that I am living on my own, being in a flat is much less lonely than inhabiting a whole house by myself.

All this does not mean there are never any arguments or disagreements. The haven of peace I hoped for in my seafront flat has been constantly disrupted by noisy neighbours, residents not on speaking terms, fierce disputes over service charges, cars being abandoned at the back, rubbish deposited in common parts, fridges, washing machines and other household goods being dumped inside and outside the building, builders' rubble languishing in the hall, leaking taps and toilets, and bitter court battles with debtors.

The Annual General Meeting has at times degenerated into a verbal Punch and Judy show.

And it is supposed to be an upmarket building!

Life in the London flat has been quieter and less full of incident but I still find I have the neighbour from hell downstairs who chainsmokes, never seems to clear out his rubbish, and who also keeps threatening to report me to the Environmental Department for employing builders who make a noise.

And I can always hear when people go in and out of the building, and when my neighbours above are in residence.

Wendy Perriam's story

In 2005, novelist Wendy Perriam moved with her husband Alan into a 9th floor flat in Dolphin Square, Central London, after spending the previous 30 years in a large detached house in Surbiton, Surrey.

Quite a life change. As regards flat living, Wendy says:

> On the plus side, living in a flat is both friendlier and easier than living in a house. I like the fact that we are now part of a community and you are always meeting people – in the lifts, on the stairs, in the gym and the swimming pool. We hardly knew who our neighbours were in Surbiton.
>
> I also like the fact we don't need a car any more, and all events, such as the theatre or ballet, are in easy distance.
>
> Also on the plus side, we don't have any maintenance in the flat, as it's all taken care of by the management company. There were always jobs to do in the house and it was endless, expensive work to keep it going.

On the minus side, says Wendy, flats are far noisier than houses and there is far less storage space.

> The kitchen is much smaller and everything has to be fitted in. We had a separate washer and tumble drier in the house, and they were both kept in an outhouse. In the flat, they have to be in the kitchen and we do not have room for a separate washer and drier. We have a washer-drier and it seems to be going all the time with no escape.
>
> When we moved here, it took months to get rid of stuff in the cellar and the attic, and I sold 870 books for 10p each. Although we spent a lot of money building bookshelves in the flat, there was never going to be enough room for all my books, or my archive material, which at the moment is in my elderly father's garage.
>
> But, decluttering gives you a good feeling. Here on the 9th floor we have wonderful views, which of course we never got with the house, but living in a flat means you have absolutely no idea of the weather, as it always seems warm in the building.
>
> So I have to go down nine floors and put my head out of the main door to know whether it's cold or hot, windy or calm.
>
> But mainly, flat living puts a different perspective on every aspect of life. It is emphatically not living in a mini-house; it is a totally different concept of living.

OTHER ASPECTS OF FLAT LIVING

Neighbour disputes are common with all types of housing, but they are intensified in flats as it is less easy to escape your tormentors. You are always likely to be meeting them at the communal front door, in the lift or the stairs. You cannot escape your neighbours in a flat as you can with a house, and there are always likely to be people not on speaking terms with each other, or somebody who makes life hell for others.

To sum up, it can be a complicated matter to live in a flat. To find out why, we will now take a look at the peculiar history of apartments and apartment living in Great Britain.

The History of Apartment Buildings

1

For most of recorded time, humans have lived in houses or, at least, in separate dwellings. Even though extended families may, at times, have lived in the same house or hut, they will always have been connected by blood or marriage. It was not the case, until fairly recently, that unconnected people lived permanently under the same roof, unless it was in an *Upstairs, Downstairs* type of situation, where some inhabitants were servants or slaves.

Flats, where everybody lives in a separate unit in the same building, and where everybody is equal, are a relatively modern invention, and can still be seen as an experiment in living that has only been partially successful. It was only really when high-density housing was needed, mainly in urban areas, that the kind of communal residential buildings we now know as flats, came into existence.

In the past, it was mainly poor people, servants and apprentices or those who had no other choice who lived in parts of houses such as attics, basements, garrets, rookeries, and very often in parts of houses not originally designed for human habitation. In any case, where attics and basements were intended for residential use, they were vastly inferior in style and construction to the rest of the house.

Most British people aspired to live in their own houses, although apartment living started to become popular in many European cities during the nineteenth century. Apartment house construction in Scotland, however, dates back to the sixteenth century, when blocks of flats were built in Edinburgh. In fact, the word 'flat' to denote a suite of rooms in a larger building comes from the Scottish word 'flaet', meaning a floor, or a storey.

In Scottish law, the term 'common interest' was used to describe the tenure rights of occupants, and enabled residents to own not only their individual apartments, but also to own rights in the common parts. This law is an early version of the co-ops and condominiums in America, where residents collectively own the building, and is very different from the leasehold laws that came to be established for British blocks of flats.

THE FIRST FLATS

The first blocks of flats to be built in Britain were in central London, and were of two very different types: housing for the affluent middle and professional classes, and housing for the very poor.

And never the twain should meet – at least, not until previously high-class apartment blocks fell into disrepair and became inhabited by squatters and the homeless.

The first upper-class blocks of flats were built in Victoria, London, in 1853. In 1886 the most prestigious apartment building of its time, Albert Hall Mansions, was completed for very well-to-do people.

In the mid-nineteenth century, what were known as 'catering flats' began to be built to offer residential accommodation to affluent people who wanted a pied-à-terre in town in addition to their country pile. The flats were aimed at single people or childless couples (not so very different from today) and some were segregated by sex, and known as 'gentlemen's apartments' or 'ladies' apartments'. The original blocks of flats aimed at the affluent were not designed for family occupation, and consisted of separate suites of rooms intended to be inhabited by people who were not related to each other and, indeed, very likely did not even know each other. As such, this was a brand new way of living, aimed at those who wanted a self-contained type of life on their own rather than be surrounded by their families, as in the past.

In the novels of Jane Austen, Dickens, Thackeray, the Brontës, George Eliot, Thomas Hardy and Anthony Trollope, nobody, but nobody, lives on their own apart from misers and those shunned by society. It was considered a terribly unnatural way to live, and not something a normally sociable person would ever want. In any case, when the only form of housing was separate houses, it was not really possible to live alone.

The advent of flats gradually changed all those perceptions, until you get to the novels of Anita Brookner, where just about all of her central characters live in solitude in a hermetically-sealed London flat.

The novelist Henry James, a lifelong celibate, lived for much of his life in one of these original central London flats in Carlyle Mansions, Cheyne Walk, Chelsea.

These early flats were luxurious for the time and were intended to combine the best of private living with hotel facilities. They consisted of self-contained suites of various sizes, where housekeeping, cleaning and catering services were often on offer. There was a common dining room where residents could eat and also billiard rooms and games rooms. All these extra services were included in the rent and initially at least it was not possible to buy or lease these suites. In time, though, residents wanted more security of tenure and began to buy leases, or long rents, from the owners.

One reason these apartments were built in the first place was to overcome the servant problem, becoming acute towards the end of the nineteenth century. These upmarket apartments did not need droves of servants, although Henry James had his faithful manservant with him, as many services were provided by the management.

Not all that popular
But in general, the demand for flats at this time was not great, and according to Norbert Schrenauer, author of the mighty tome *6000 Years of Housing*, there were two main reasons for this: fear of the spread of infection from such close living, and the problem of noise. Apparently, too, the innate conservatism of the building industry at the time meant that developers tended to stick to the more traditional type of housing.

Also, British people continued to resist flat living where they had the choice, preferring their own house, however humble, with its own front door and garden, than life in an anonymous block of flats.

HOUSING FOR THE POOR

There were, though, other apartment buildings going up in mid-Victorian times, and these were aimed at a quite different sector of the population from Albert Hall Mansions and the like: the urban poor, or very poor.

Flats for these people were built by philanthropists such as Peabody and Guinness, and indeed, you can still see antiquated-looking buildings bearing the names Peabody Buildings and Guinness Buildings in ornate Victorian lettering, in many parts of London.

The first apartment building of this type was opened on February 29, 1864 in Spitalfields, in the East End of London, by the American philanthropist George Peabody.

The building consisted of seven tenements of three rooms at five shillings (25p) a week; 42 tenements of two rooms at four shillings (20p) a week; six tenements of two rooms at 3/6 (15½p) a week, and two tenements of one room at 2/6 (12½p) a week.

The living rooms in these early tenements measured 13' by 10' and the ceilings were eight feet high. Staircases and corridors were lit by gas fixtures and there were laundries on the top floor. There were no bathrooms in the individual tenements but lavatories on every floor. There was also the unimaginable luxury that hot baths were available simply by asking the superintendent for a key.

These tenements were intended for poor people 'of good character' and were highly innovative for the time. The rents, at least in the Peabody Buildings, were set 'at cost' which meant that they simply covered what the building cost to run, with no profits for anybody.

Also in Victorian times, what we now know as maisonettes were built for working-class people in large industrial towns such as Newcastle-upon-Tyne and Liverpool. These maisonettes consisted of a separate upstairs and downstairs in a long terrace, with two front doors side by side. One family would live upstairs and the other, downstairs, but be completely separate from each other. Even the back yards at the rear of the property were separate, so that each family had complete privacy, even though living literally on top of each other.

My first married home was one of these maisonettes and consisted of three bedrooms, one living room, a tiny kitchen and bathroom and dingy backyard. The rent in 1965 for this unfurnished upstairs maisonette was £3.10s (£3.50) a week. Not long ago, a friend returned to the area and said the street was completely unspoilt, by which he meant unmodernised. These maisonettes now mainly house social tenants.

In the 1920s and 30s, more blocks of flats were built by philanthropists for the urban poor, but the aspiration was still to have a complete house rather than live in a flat.

MOVING ON
In the 1940s, especially just after the Second World War, councils and local authorities started building blocks of flats, again often very innovative for their time.

The 'children's laureate', writer Jacqueline Wilson, has recalled
how she went to live with her family in a council flat in Kingston,
Surrey, in the 1950s and could not believe the luxury – there was
hot water on tap, central heating and a bathroom ... these were all
amenities which were certainly not automatic in working-class
housing at the time.

Also around this time, existing houses in areas such as Notting
Hill, West London, had pretty much fallen into disrepair, and
were bought cheaply by slum landlords with the idea of turning
them into nasty flats for poor people and immigrants. These
cheap rented dwellings gave flats a bad name. One such dwelling,
10 Rillington Place, was a dismal, dilapidated tiny terrace house
badly converted into three flats. On the top floor lived Beryl and
Timothy Evans and on the bottom floor, the serial killer John
Christie. After Christie left the flat, some West Indians, recent
immigrants, moved in and noticed a strange, very nasty smell in
the place. It came from decomposing bodies walled up in the
kitchen. The new tenants called the police and Christie was
eventually hanged for the murder of at least five women. Soon
after this, Rillington Place was pulled down and the street was
renamed Ruston Mews. But until it was comprehensively
gentrified in the 1980s and 90s, Notting Hill was full of these slum
flats and, indeed, was notorious for them.

During the 1950s and 60s, council flats continued to be built but by
this time, they tended to be tower blocks, which initially seemed a
good idea but the high-rise soon became synonymous with sink
estates. Although the term high-rise is one of approbation in
America, in the UK it is now always used pejoratively.

Until the mid-twentieth century, with the grand exception of the imposing mansion blocks in places like Knightsbridge and Belgravia, flats were very much seen as housing for poor people who could not afford a proper house. The 1960s song, 'My old man's a dustman/ He wears a dustman's hat/ He wears gorblimey trousers/ and he lives in a council flat' summed up the prevailing conception of council flats being the very lowest in housing options.

But before long, luxury blocks of flats were being built which were aimed at professional people. These luxury flats tended to be in ultra-desirable locations where it was no longer possible or affordable to have separate houses. One of my early boyfriends, in the 1960s, lived with his parents in a modern flat overlooking Kew Gardens. This seemed to me very glamorous, as I had never before known anybody who lived in a flat.

Also in the 1960s, 'bachelor flats' or what we would now call studio flats, were designed to give single people self-contained places of their own. Before this, as we read in the novels of Barbara Pym, single working people of limited or ordinary means had to resort to 'rooms' where they would often have to share bathrooms and kitchens.

FLAT LIVING BECOMES STYLISH

Although as the twentieth century progressed, more people in London started living in flats, owing to considerations of space and money, prevailing attitudes towards flat living only started to improve in the mid-1990s, when ever smarter and trendier apartment blocks began to be constructed. The buy-to-let phenomenon, plus advances in building technology, meant that flats were, finally, becoming highly desirable and, in many cases, more desirable than houses.

For just as apartment buildings of the nineteenth century had laundries, games rooms, common dining rooms and lifts – all very innovative for the time – so present-day apartments also usher in many new ideas in housing. The more luxurious buildings now offer spas, gyms, 24-hour concierge services, underground valet parking and swimming pools, whereas the Peabody Trust is now opting for modular, prefabricated housing which provides cheap, contemporary flats.

The Peabody Trust, for instance, developed a new concept of modular housing in 1998 in Murray Grove, Hackney, where the finished apartments were available at cost rent, adhering to the original Peabody principle. The Murray Grove building is aimed at young singles and couples who cannot afford a mortgage but who do not qualify for social housing. Needless to say, the demand is huge.

THE PROBLEMS OF TENURE

So far as Britons were concerned, there was always an inherent problem with the tenure of apartments, for those not content merely to rent week by week. It was this factor, really, which militated most against flat living becoming truly desirable. The original council flats, mansion-block apartments and Peabody-type buildings were all rented rather than owned.

At time went on, it was really the problems with tenure and ownership which prevented more people from buying flats, as few understood the ramifications of leasehold. Most people who had a choice did not like the idea of leasehold, as this was very much seen as a kind of second-best way of owning, and not the real thing at all.

By contrast, everybody understood what freehold meant and where they could, people preferred to buy a freehold property they would own in perpetuity.

Where council flats were concerned, everything changed anyway with the right-to-buy ushered in by Mrs Thatcher in the 1980s, where former council tenants could buy their lease at a massive discount, and then sell it on if they wished after living there for a minimum of three years. Thus, council flats went onto the open market in the late 1980s, and soon began to compete with private housing, as these flats were often in excellent locations. Most of these original leases were for 125 years and, indeed still are, for council tenants buying long leases.

Although it was relatively easy for a local authority to sell separate houses, establishing leases for council flats for previous tenants who wished to buy, was complicated, as it meant there would be a mixture of leaseholders and tenants in the same block. These problems have still not been fully ironed out, and make buying a former council property a more difficult endeavour than buying a flat in the private sector.

A CONTINUING PROBLEM

What we now understand as leasehold law developed piecemeal as more people became interested in buying their flats or, at least, in buying a long lease. But our complicated system goes back to the Norman Conquest, when William the Conqueror annexed all the land in the country for himself.

William declared that all the land belonged to him and then gave it away to his followers in return for services to the king.

These new landholders were originally known as tenants and their holdings, as tenures. Lords who held land from the king in time divided up their holdings and parcelled it out to subordinate tenants, who also owed them some kind of service. This is how the feudal land laws, remnants of which remain in place to this day, came into existence and eventually affected modern leasehold flats.

The point about tenure is that the landholder did not absolutely own the land but derived right of possession from somebody else, and for a specified time. During the Middle Ages, there were three types of ownership in existence: 'estate in fee simple'; 'estate in fee tail' and 'life estate'.

The types of ownership

Briefly, the first type of ownership meant that land could be inherited by the owner's male heirs according to the system of primogeniture; the second type of ownership meant that there was an identified line of succession outside which the land could not be transferred, and the third simply lasted for the life of the tenant, and ended on his death.

Part of the plot of Jane Austen's *Pride and Prejudice* hinges on the concept of entail; Mrs Bennet wants Elizabeth to marry the ghastly Mr Collins because the estate is entailed and would pass directly to him on Mr Bennet's death. Be that as it may, no Bennet daughter was prepared to marry Mr Collins for the sake of securing the property.

Nowadays, the only vestige of the old land laws is the 'estate in fee simple' which means in effect that if you buy a house which stands on its own land, you will own that piece of property in perpetuity, or until you come to sell. That is what is meant nowadays by freehold. But if you own an apartment, say on the third floor of a block, you cannot own the freehold because your property does not stand directly on the land.

The term leasehold, which denotes the number of years remaining on the lease, is in many ways a lingering reminder of the old feudal system which meant that after the number of years was up, the land or estate reverted to the lord.

But the old idea that property eventually belongs to the Crown persists in the fact that if leasehold buildings which have become limited companies do not make proper annual returns to Companies House, the whole thing can revert to ownership by the Crown and individual leaseholders lose everything.

REFORMING LAWS

The Law of Property Act, 1925, was an attempt to rationalise land laws and bring them in tune with modern times and reflect modern usage. But although much was done to sweep away the old feudal laws, the concepts of freehold and leasehold became enshrined in the new laws. In most other countries, you can buy the freehold of an apartment and still own the land on which it is built, through the system of co-operative ownership.

For some reason though, British governments have never quite succeeded in doing away with old leasehold laws where you can't buy your flat but only a length of tenure.

It is true that there are some freehold flats in this country, but they are a legal fiction, and never worth very much on the open market. This is because mortgage lenders are reluctant to lend money on a property which does not conform to known laws, as they fear they will not be able to repossess should the mortgagee fall into arrears.

But as flat living becomes ever more the norm, leaseholders are acquiring more security of tenure. When relatively few people lived in flats, it was not really worth the government's time reforming the laws, but now things have changed.

Present-day leaseholders can collectively enfranchise, which means they can buy the freehold from the landlord. Individually leaseholders have the right to extend their lease to 90 years, at a 'reasonable' cost, and they can exercise the Right to Manage, without having to prove any dereliction on the part of the freeholder or managing agents.

THE HISTORY OF SERVICE CHARGES

Service charges are always a bone of contention in blocks of flats as nobody likes paying them. At first the whole system seems unfair. You, the leaseholder, buy the lease, and then have to keep paying for repairs when you never own the place.

This does not happen if you are an ordinary tenant on an Assured Shorthold Tenancy, so why does it happen when you buy a lease?

When people first began to live in apartment buildings, they almost always rented from the landlord or freeholder. This rent would include all services, often including what we would now call utility bills, such as for heating, lighting and water.

But then, as time went on, occupants wanted more security of tenure, and so leases began to be offered – 5 years, 10 years, 20 years and so on. As leases lengthened, occupants started to sell these leases, or what was left on them, to others.

Once leases began to be sold on the open market, money was no longer paid to the landlord, but to the outgoing leaseholder. This meant that the freeholder would now have no income from selling the leases and no way of funding the running of the building.

So service charges were introduced, whereby all leaseholders had to pay an annual amount to the freeholder for running the place, otherwise it would rapidly fall into disrepair.

But as nobody liked paying service charges and everybody almost always thought they were too high, ways had to be formulated both for ensuring that service charges were paid and, also, that freeholders were not unduly profiting from their leaseholders.

Then as time went on, the original freeholders died or sold on the freehold to others, and, in this way, leasehold law and flat living gradually became ridiculously complicated. Half the time, leaseholders had no idea who the freeholder was. It could be an individual, a company or a consortium, even an insurance or finance company.

Then, original leases began to run down and lose their value. So, again, a way had to be found of ensuring that long leaseholders could continue to live in their homes. That was when the right to a lease extension came in.

Variables

These are the variables that can exist in a block of flats:

- Leaseholders with an outside freeholder.
- Leaseholders with a share of the freehold who have formed a company limited by guarantee.
- Outside managing agents.
- There is a head leaseholder below the freeholder.
- The block is self-managed.
- There is a Residents' Association.
- There are some leaseholders and some tenants paying monthly rent (ex-local authority blocks).
- There may be many absentee landlords subletting.
- In rare cases, the flats themselves may be freehold.
- The building may be Commonhold.
- The leases may all be the same.
- The leases may be very different from each other.
- There may be leaseholders with wildly varying lengths of lease left.
- There may be a sinking fund.
- There may be no sinking fund.
- The block may be well run.
- The block may be badly run.
- With some new blocks, the tenure may be something new – commonhold.

Many people still see flats as types of cheap houses, without really understanding that in effect, when they buy a flat, they are buying into a morass of complications which often even the most astute legal brains fail to untangle satisfactorily.

And none of the above remotely apply when you buy a house. You just buy the house and that's it. And just to make things even more complicated, there are very many types of flats you can buy.

2

What Type of Flat is it Best to Buy?

Depending on your price range, location and preference, there are a large number of options available when buying an apartment. You will have usually far more choice than when buying a house.

You can buy new, old, trendy and contemporary or grand and traditional apartments. A small or large apartment, perhaps on the ground floor or a penthouse.

Obviously, you want to buy a flat that will, with any luck, increase in value over time, but apart from the considerations of the length of the lease, management structure and leasehold/freehold issues, there is still a lot to think about.

EXPLORING THE TYPES OF FLAT AVAILABLE

There are very many types of apartments on offer, such as:

- conversion
- mansion block
- purpose-built block
- maisonette
- newbuild
- warehouse or other conversion from former non-residential premises
- ex-local authority block
- small block
- large block

- flats over shops
- shell apartments
- shared ownership
- live/work units
- retirement or 'age exclusive' apartments.

We will take a look at each of these in turn.

CONVERSION

These are most often Victorian or Georgian conversions, cut-downs from a bigger house, although they can also be Edwardian or 1930s semis, if large enough.

Advantages

There are not usually many apartments in each house, possibly five or six maximum. Conversions also usually have low service charges and are frequently sold with a share of the freehold. Because of the small number of units in each house, you are unlikely to get the level of administrative problems which can occur in larger blocks. Most conversions are in urban locations, and enable you to live in an area you might not otherwise be able to afford.

Newspaper stories of former broom cupboards being sold as studio apartments in very expensive areas such as Knightsbridge and Chelsea, for instance, remind us that these tiny conversions enable buyers with very small budgets to live in self-contained apartments in trendy and central locations.

If location is more important than size, then you are most likely to find what you are looking for in a conversion.

Disadvantages

In older conversions, some of the rooms may be tiny, such as kitchens and bathrooms. Also the conversion may have been done amateurishly before present day building regulations were in force. Because walls can be thin, conversions are often very noisy places to live in.

Very often, common parts are dilapidated and rundown and there are likely to be areas nobody bothers about, especially if all the residents jointly own the freehold. When I lived in a conversion, there was a cupboard at the top of one landing that seemed to belong to nobody; consequently it was full of rubbish, and none of the residents would take the responsibility of clearing it out.

In most conversions, the apartments are far from being equal in size or grandeur. There will usually be one grand flat, which constituted the family's living quarters in Victorian days, and then as you go upstairs, the flats get smaller and less well appointed, as they were usually the original servants' quarters.

This inequality can lead to disputes over apportionment of the service charges, especially as such conversions are usually too small to make it worth bothering with managing agents. It is most usual for one of the residents to take responsibility for management; or, as happened in my case, we took it in turns.

Conversions work well when everybody gets on, as we did, but they can be a nightmare if you have a problem or non-paying neighbour.

Common parts tend to be small and narrow landings and halls from the former house. So there is often nowhere to put bikes, for instance, which means they are found in the hall and this can look messy and depressing. There may also be problems with parking, especially where there are now four or five homes in what was formerly a single dwelling.

MANSION BLOCK

These, the first 'purpose built' blocks date back to late Victorian and early Edwardian days and are often extremely grand and imposing.

Advantages

As the flats are not cut-downs from a whole house, they are not subject to the inequalities of size that happens in conversions. Also, as they were originally built to be flats, there is less danger of the gimcrack kind of adaptation you can find in conversions.

Although the individual flats in mansion blocks may be of varying sizes, they were all at least intended to be flats, right from the start. Common parts tend to be well kept, there is often a resident porter or caretaker, and a contractor employed to clean windows and maintain the exterior. Communal gardens are usually also very well kept. Mansion blocks tend to be found in central locations in big cities.

Other advantages are that they have high ceilings and the rooms are a good size.

Disadvantages

There may be an antiquated communal heating and hot water system in place, and this hikes up service charges. These tend to be high anyway with mansion blocks, as there are often luxurious carpets and expensive wallpaper in common parts. The décor is often extremely traditional. There may not be a car park or any parking facilities as these blocks were often built before cars were invented.

Many residents will have been living there for decades, and if a large number are pensioners, it can be difficult to collect money for the major repairs which mansion blocks will certainly need from time to time.

Another disadvantage is that drainage and plumbing systems were put in before the days of power showers, en suite bathrooms, dishwashers and washing machines, so often the existing system cannot cope and has to be redone at huge expense. Leaks are common in mansion blocks and it may be difficult to discover their origin.

Also, many mansion blocks are huge, dark and forbidding, especially in London, and you may never get to know your neighbours.

PURPOSE-BUILT BLOCKS

These were built from the 1930s, as the demand for apartments increased, and many, such as the art deco Embassy Court in Brighton, have now become listed buildings. They have a very different look from the Edwardian mansion blocks, which are usually redbrick and very ornate.

Purpose-built (PB) blocks are more modest in appearance, although they again often have resident porters and well maintained, if more modest, common parts than mansion blocks.

Advantages
As with the mansion blocks, they are not cut-downs from bigger houses, so each flat is usually a decent size. Again, they tend to be in very central locations, and enable you to live in a location where you might not be able to afford a whole house.

Security is usually excellent, and the block will almost always be managed by professional managing agents. PB blocks may or may not come with a share of the freehold but these days there will almost always be a residents' association which keeps a close eye on expenditure and the upkeep of the fabric.

Disadvantages
As with mansion blocks, the older PB blocks often have communal central heating and hot water. This not only hikes up the service charges, but means you cannot control their operations. Consequently you can be boiling in October when the central heating is turned on, and freezing in May, when it is turned off. Also, as everybody in the block is likely to be having a bath or shower at more or less the same time, the 'hot' water can at times be tepid or even cold.

It is usually too expensive and difficult to untangle the pipework so that everybody can put in an individual system. These communal systems usually date back to the 1960s, after which individual systems were put in using Combi boilers.

Flats in PB blocks can seem suspiciously cheap and there are good reasons for this; high service charges and, often, high prices to be paid for lease extensions. In some older PB blocks, leases can be very short, as well.

NEWBUILDS

These are springing up all over the place and often incorporate trendy new features enabling luxury living at a fraction of the cost of buying a house in a similar location.

Advantages

Even quite modestly-priced apartments in new blocks are often sold with fitted kitchens, bathrooms, carpets and curtains included in the price. If you get in early, you can usually choose your carpets, worktop finish and tiling from a range. Security is tight and there may well be an underground car park, gym, spa, swimming pool, laundry and dry cleaning facilities and possibly even an art gallery or shops. Locations are usually excellent, as newbuilds tend to be constructed where there are good transport links. From the higher flats, views may be stunning.

There will also be a 10-year building certificate in place. Soundproofing is usually excellent, and many new design features will be incorporated.

Disadvantages

Newbuilds are very heavily marketed, with beautifully-designed showhomes to gawp at, plus 'incentives' such as your stamp duty paid or a 'guaranteed six per cent rental' if you intend to rent out the apartment. And sometimes there may be a cash incentive on top of all this. If you buy offplan at an early stage, you can also often secure what seems like a massive discount.

But beware! Developers are not primarily in the business of giving you money, but making money for themselves. There may be hidden disincentives if you look hard, such as the flat not being sold with a share of the freehold, and service charges being hiked up after a couple of years of being kept artificially low.

In addition, there are often a lot of investor buyers with newbuilds, often from consortia in Hong Kong or somewhere who buy up many apartments in the block at a huge discount. So there may be many absentee landlords renting out properties, which means a large transient population. In one newbuild block in London, a single investor bought up 26 units at a stroke, all to rent out.

Also, there are many property clubs in existence which purport to sell newbuild flats for a discounted price, at an early stage of the construction. Many people nowadays are 'buying to flip' which means they never intend to live there themselves or even rent the place out, but to sell straight on at a profit. This can mean a lot of empty flats when you move in; some buy-to-flip flats can take two or three years to sell. In the meantime, they stay empty with permanent 'For Sale' notices which look dreary and depressing, and as if everybody has cynically bought as an investment rather than a home.

With a newbuild, it may take a long time to recoup the investment and you may also be living surrounded by rubble and building works, as apartments are 'released' usually in phases, long before the development is fully completed. There is also likely to be a long snagging list, even with the building certificate in place. The first people into a new block often find many things go wrong as the place has not been tried and tested.

You may also discover that you buy into a trendy, contemporary apartment which starts to look distinctly old-fashioned after a few years. Many newbuilds are sold with kitchens and bathrooms already in place, and with kitchens this usually means black granite or other feature which will inevitably, like the latest fashion in clothes, have a fixed life, after which it will look horribly dated.

Ceilings tend to be low in newbuilds, and windows are usually plastic (UPVC) which start to look distinctly dingy after a few years.

Developers often sell on the freehold upon completion, which can mean insecurity about who will eventually own the place. Also, it takes time for residents' associations to be formed; this can be difficult if there are many investors buying, either to flip or to rent out. Only owner-occupiers will be interested in forming such associations.

TIP

A note on 'discounts': they are not always what they appear. One buyer was told that a two-bedroom newbuild was on the market at £220,000, but because she belonged to a property club, she could buy it a discount for £193,000. However, it was valued by a local estate agent at £173,000 – and she couldn't even sell it at that price.

WAREHOUSE CONVERSIONS

These are rapidly turning into trendy homes and are extremely popular for 'loft living'. Most often, these are new conversions from buildings not originally intended to be for residential use, such as old police stations, factories, industrial units, fire stations, post offices, schools, colleges and barns and outbuildings.

Advantages

Large spaces and central locations, plus a definite style cachet, make these apartments very popular.

Disadvantages

They can look barn-like and forbidding, and are often sold in an unfinished state, so you will have to do a lot of the work yourself, which can be costly and time-consuming. Loft and barn conversions can be difficult to make cosy.

EX-LOCAL AUTHORITY BLOCKS

A lot of flats in these blocks have come onto the open market since the original buyers, former council tenants who bought at a huge discount under Mrs Thatcher's right to buy scheme, have sold and moved on. At one time, flats in these blocks were distinctly cheaper than others; now, depending on location and the condition of the estate, they often go for much the same price as any other flat of a comparable size.

Advantages

The flats are often surprisingly roomy, with good storage and big, square rooms. In addition, they are often in excellent locations, and have well-kept communal gardens.

Service charges are usually low, when compared to comparable private flats in similar locations. Very often there will be a balcony which gives at least some outside space.

Security is usually good and caretaking services are provided in the service charges. Also, rubbish is collected regularly.

The buildings are looked after by the local council, so there are rarely serious management problems. Also, nobody is making a profit as in the private sector, as local councils are not allowed to make a profit.

Disadvantages

They can be on rundown estates. These blocks rarely have any architectural features of merit, and can look forbidding and offputting, even if inside they are often a pleasant surprise.

If buying into a high-rise or tower block, leases can be short and it may be difficult to extend, which means it is impossible to get a mortgage. There will be little or no resale value if you buy on a short lease higher than the seventh floor.

Common parts and lifts may be covered in graffiti or vandalised. Values are unlikely to increase significantly even with a long lease on a first or second floor flat where there is a high proportion of council tenants, homeless or rehoused people.

You are buying into mixed tenure. In the majority of ex-local authority blocks, there will be a mix of leaseholders, tenants of leaseholders, property investors and social tenants. This means that these blocks tend to have a lower value than in the private sector.

Service charges usually seem low and this is because local authorities are not allowed to amass a sinking fund. This means that whenever major repairs are indicated, you are charged for your percentage share under the lease, which could come to four or five figures unexpectedly.

Even when the common parts are clean and tidy, they are rarely warm or welcoming, as most council blocks were originally built as cheaply as possible.

SMALL BLOCKS

Apartment buildings vary enormously in size, from a two-maisonette building to a very large block containing four or five hundred flats. As ever, the definition of a 'flat' is where you share roof and foundations, and possibly, some external walls.

A 'small block' is usually one where there are six or fewer units in the building.

Advantages

With small blocks, you almost always know your neighbours, there is no real need for outside management adding to the running costs, and provided you are all neighbourly, you can sort out repair and maintenance matters amicably and without fuss. Small blocks are necessarily cheaper to run than large blocks; you may not need to employ outside caretaking and cleaning services and will probably not have to go to the expense of a lift.

Disadvantages

Small blocks can be a nightmare where there are feuding neighbours, or one owner who refuses to co-operate. Also, you are not likely to enjoy the amenities of a large block such as underground carpark, communal gardens or a gym, for instance.

LARGE BLOCKS

By far the great majority of newbuilds are large blocks, as these are more cost-effective for developers. But there are also many large blocks dating back to Victorian and Edwardian days, and every decade up to the present time. Large blocks can contain several hundred individual apartments.

Advantages

You can be more anonymous in a large block; this is an advantage for some, but a disadvantage for others. There is likely to be better security and cleaning arrangements in a large block and of course, there is a greater choice of properties within the block. Neighbour disputes tend to be less personal, and as flats are frequently changing hands in a large block, even quite serious disputes do not usually last long.

It is easier to club together and buy the freehold in a large block, to exercise the Right to Manage, and to form a Residents' Association. In a large block, there is safety in numbers!

Disadvantages

Large blocks cost far more to run than small blocks, so service charges will be higher. Large apartment buildings can also be forbidding, and repairs expensive and difficult to carry out as they almost always need scaffolding. There will often be at least one or two debtors and vexatious owners in a large block. Large blocks also definitely need outside managing agents, and this also hikes up the cost of service charges.

The older the block, the more likely it is to have fallen into at least some disrepair, and need major renovation or updating. Lifts in large blocks, for instance, can be very expensive to repair or replace.

FLATS OVER SHOPS

In recent years, the government has been trying to persuade people to invest in flats over shops, which have historically had a bad reputation.

Advantages
Such flats are usually in excellent locations, as they are in shopping areas, and being over a shop means they are cheaper to buy than a comparable flat not over a shop.

Disadvantages
The lease situation will usually involve the shop, and be complicated, as it is part-commercial and part-residential. This means the landlord is very likely to be a company or corporation, rather than a person. You will have no say in the kind of shop you are over, and if you are over commercial premises which turns into an off-licence, betting shop or charity shop, your flat may lose value.

Flats over shops are less easy to sell than others, and often have extremely dismal, dilapidated common parts and nasty doors. Common parts also tend to be very dark and poorly lit.

SHELL APARTMENTS

These are sold as 'shells' where in effect you buy an empty space already marked out as a flat, but possibly without already being divided into rooms. There may not be a kitchen, bathrooms, flooring or any storage when you buy the apartment. In a way, shell apartments are the complete opposite to standard newbuilds, which come ready with fully-fitted kitchens and bathrooms, carpets and other flooring.

Advantages

Shell apartments are almost always in large cities and unlike warehouse conversions, which they resemble in some ways, tend to be built from scratch. They are usually large, and mean you can totally stamp your own personality on your home, which can be difficult with the average newbuild apartment. Shell apartments can be made to look strikingly individual.

Disadvantages

It can be difficult to budget, as obviously everything you put in will be at extra cost to yourself, and it may also be difficult to visualise exactly what it will look like when finished. Shell apartments are usually aimed at the high end of the market and will be expensive in the first place.

It can also be hard to make these apartments look cosy.

You need to have quite a lot of the interior designer and architect about you to make a shell apartment work successfully.

SHARED OWNERSHIP

In this case, you buy part of an apartment and rent the other part. You can buy with up to four other people, and buy a share on which you can get a mortgage. You then pay ordinary rent for the remaining share that you do not own. As time goes on, you can increase your share and eventually own your home outright. Mainly, the owners are housing associations or other social landlords or non-profit organisations, and this part-rent, part-buy scheme is seen as a way of helping those on low incomes onto the property ladder. In effect, you buy your home in stages.

Buyers must be considered to be in housing need who cannot afford the price of properties for sale on the open market.

Once you have bought a share, however, you will become responsible for service charges and a share of any renovation work on the building.

This type of housing is often known as 'affordable' or 'key worker' housing.

Advantages
This is a good way for young people of limited means to get into property ownership and in exchange for buying a share, you will be given a lease of, typically, 99 years.

There is high demand for these units and you will not usually find it difficult to sell your share, or the property outright if you have acquired 100 per cent of the shares.

Disadvantages
You are neither one thing nor the other; neither a real renter nor a real owner and, in some ways, can experience the disadvantages of both. And unless you own the property outright, you may have

to sell your share to a prospective buyer nominated by the social landlord. In some areas, the social landlord may also restrict your ability to buy further shares in your home, and may reserve the right to buy back the property from you.

You must also obtain permission from the landlord to carry out any internal improvements or alterations.

LIVE/WORK UNITS

These are a relatively new idea, and refer to a combination of living and working units in a single, purpose-designed type of accommodation. This idea is very different from working from home, as the workspace will be a dedicated commercial unit.

Live/work units can be a good idea for people who are setting up their first business and may not be able to obtain separate finance for business premises.

So far as tax is concerned, live/work is not currently a recognised term, and is classified under the old-fashioned phrase 'composite hereditament'. This means it contains both domestic and non-domestic property, but there must be some domestic use involved. Live/work units cannot just be regarded as cheap offices.

The part of the unit used for living is rated under ordinary council tax bands, and the work area will be charged under business rates. A Valuation Officer will have to come round in each case and make an assessment.

You can get either a residential mortgage, a commercial mortgage or a mixture of the two. In normal cases, live/work units are mortgageable in the same way as ordinary residential units.

Advantages

The advantages are obvious! You can live and work in the same space, yet have clearly defined areas for each activity, so you are not running a business on your kitchen table. Ordinary leases do not normally allow businesses to be run from residential premises, so these units are a breakthrough. Most live/work units are sold on leases of at least 100 years and the ground rents and service charges applicable are very similar to those of ordinary residential apartments.

Disadvantages

Well, you can never escape from your work or shut the door on the office and go home, because your home and office are in the same space. There may well be restrictions on the type of business you can run from such a unit, or whether you can have employees, and it may be difficult to expand your business as there is nowhere for it to go.

The Capital Gains Tax situation could be difficult when you come to sell, as you will be liable for the business part of the property and not for the living part.

You would also have to sell your unit to another live/work buyer, so it could take longer to sell than a purely residential unit and is also unlikely to increase in value as much as a fully residential property.

RETIREMENT/AGE EXCLUSIVE APARTMENTS

Nowadays, there is a huge choice of apartments aimed at older people, from the simple 'age exclusive' home where you have to be, typically, 50 or over to buy into the development, to whole estates which offer a full range of hospital and nursing services.

Retirement homes come at every end of the market, from exclusive apartments in gated developments to cheap mass-produced housing.

Many retirement homes also have visitor suites which you can book, communal dining and games rooms, and a warden or concierge on duty. Most also have a 'panic button' which you can press for immediate medical assistance.

Retirement apartments are the fastest growing sector of the housing market and, for the developers at least, one of the most profitable.

Advantages

As these apartments are purpose-built for older people, they will often have wider doors than usual, for wheelchair use, easy-access bathrooms and other features designed to make life easy for older and less able people.

Disadvantages

All your neighbours are old or elderly! My former mother-in-law, who ended her days in a sheltered home, complained that everybody around her was deaf, and she missed the lively chatter and mobility of younger people. The biggest disadvantage, however luxurious the development, is perhaps this 'ghetto' aspect.

Service charges tend to be high, as there are more services than usual provided in these homes, and locations are not always as good as they might be. In many instances, you have to pay a premium back to the developers when you sell, and in any case you cannot sell on the open market; only to other qualifying people.

Some retirement apartments are very small and dark, while others can be truly luxurious. This all depends on your pocket.

Only reasonably active older people are allowed in sheltered accommodation, as if you need round-the-clock or hospital care, you will not be allowed to buy. Originally, most sheltered homes had live-in wardens, but few do now, and most have assistants who come in only for a couple of hours or so a day.

IS THERE A BEST BUY?

Probably not, as each type of flat has its particular pros and cons.

The only way to look at the situation is to ask whether you can see yourself living in the place, and fitting into its existing structure. Some older people, for instance, would not dream of going into 'age-exclusive' apartments, while for others it is a wonderful luxury to be in a flat designed with their needs in mind.

For some people, price is the main criterion, whereas for others, space or nearness to main transport links, shops and theatres will take precedence. One friend has a gorgeous flat in Covent Garden which is above commercial premises. She is near to everything, but there is nowhere at all to park.

There is no such thing as a wonderful apartment which has all the advantages and none of the disadvantages, so you have to ask yourself how important, for instance, are architectural features or a period feel against convenience or low service charges.

I would say these are the main aspects to look out for when considering which flat to buy:

Parking provision

This is particularly important in large cities, as if the entire building is on double yellow lines with nowhere to park, you will be forever driving round the area. If there is a garage priced as an extra, as is often the case, go for it.

Most modern blocks of flats are built with underground parking; pre-1960s blocks are unlikely to have this facility and ex-local authority blocks almost never offer it.

Neat and tidy common parts

This indicates the building is well run and that most service charges are paid on time. First impressions count when you to go to view a flat.

A caretaker

In very large blocks, the caretaker may live in. There should always be somebody in charge of caretaking, rather than relying on contract cleaners.

Cleanliness of windows and type of curtains

This is maybe your biggest indicator of the type of neighbours you will have under the roof. Dingy, yellowing, nicotine-stained net curtains, filthy broken windows and cardboard or sacking up at the windows should all be your signals to steer well clear.

Condition of the exterior
This also indicates whether there is enough money being raised, or raisable, to keep the building in good repair.

The state of communal gardens, porches and driveways
Again, the cleaner and smarter these are, the more you can buy with confidence.

Other points
From experience, I would say that one thing to avoid is communal heating and hot water systems which are not only fiendishly expensive, but are always going wrong. And the hotness of the water is never guaranteed.

Buying with a share of the freehold, although often recommended, can also have its problems as very often, residents argue among themselves. Both Lease and the Citizens Advice Bureau say that neighbour disputes in blocks of flats have greatly increased since collective enfranchisement became popular.

WHERE IN THE BLOCK?
The choice does not end with deciding on the type of flat you prefer. There is also a choice of storey: you can live at the top, in the basement, on the ground floor, or go for a garden flat.

Best buy
Is there a best buy here?

Most definitely. I would always recommend buying a first- or second-floor flat, with a balcony. You can easily get cabin fever when contained in a flat, especially at weekends, and even a little outside space such as a balcony or patio makes a world of difference.

I would tend to avoid a ground floor flat, especially where you are at street level, as you are then subject to all the noises and possible vandalism of the street. You are also liable to be disturbed by the front door continually opening and shutting, and the sound of other people's doorbells. If your flat opens straight into the hall, there will be comings and goings which are not noticed on other levels.

The only flats that come with gardens, apart from roof gardens, will be at ground floor or basement level and here you have to offset the disadvantages of being on this level, with the advantage of outside space. Do not buy a basement flat with no outside space; it is like living in a prison. In older buildings, it can be difficult to get rid of damp in a basement.

The highest premiums are, of course, reserved for penthouse flats, particularly where these have a stunning view and perhaps a roof garden. Penthouse flats can easily go for twice as much as others in the same block, and increase in value more quickly. Of course, penthouse flats are only popular in buildings with a lift. Few people want to trudge up six or seven flights of stairs and you may have trouble getting tradesmen to deliver without a lift.

Wherever possible, go for a flat with a view as these also command a premium price.

TIP

If you are buying a flat with the intention of letting it out rather than living in it yourself, exactly the same strictures apply. In general, tenants value the same things that owners value and even as an absentee owner, you will still want to know that your purchase will gain, not lose, value over time.

As ever, the most fundamental aspect of buying a flat is *the lease*. We will now take a look at the ramifications and complications of this often troublesome document.

3

The Lease

The lease is by far the most important aspect of any flat purchase, as it governs the behaviour both of residents and the freeholder, if there is an outside freeholder. Even if there is not, and the lease is sold with a share of the freehold, there will still be a 'leaseholder' and a 'freeholder' or 'landlord', even if the leaseholders and landlords are one and the same.

In situations where the residents have enfranchised, the landlord will have become a limited company, so that if the building is called Fairview Court, the landlord will be Fairview Court Ltd, where each resident is a shareholder and there is a Board of Directors and a Secretary.

There has to be some kind of separation into freeholder and leaseholder for the thing to work, to ensure that service charges are met, common parts are looked after and repairs are carried out. Even when the 'lunatics run the asylum', there has to be some legally-binding document in place that ensures the smooth running of the building.

There may or may not be managing agents, as this is not a legal requirement. But, in any case, the limited company acting as the landlord has the same powers as an outside landlord, and can forfeit leases or put a charge on a property.

Now you can see how it becomes complicated to buy a flat! The lease is a legally binding document on both sides, and there could be serious penalties for breaches. When you sign a lease, you enter into the terms of that lease, so it is as well to know what you are signing.

QUESTIONS TO ASK

If you are interested in a lovely flat in a wonderful location you need to ask – and have satisfactory answers to – the following questions before ever making an offer:

1. How long is the lease? Very often, on estate agents' particulars, it says 'to be advised'. They want to get you through the door before they tell you the bad news, by which time, they hope, you will have fallen irrevocably in love with the flat. Be very careful of properties where the lease is 80 years or less, as it will then be difficult to obtain a mortgage. And even more difficult to sell!

2. Is the flat being sold with a share of the freehold? Nowadays, estate agents often put this on the particulars, but not always. Always buy with a share of the freehold where possible, as this means there is no outsider in overall charge.

3. If the flat is *not* sold with a share of the freehold, who is the landlord or freeholder? Is anything known about this person or company? Do they generally have a good reputation? It is important to remember that estate agents do not always know themselves who is the landlord, so it is up to you to find out, especially if they look blank when you ask them.

4. Is there more than one leaseholder? In other words, is there a complicated layer of ownership where there is a landlord, a head leaseholder and ordinary leaseholders, such as you, the buyer? This often happens with mansion blocks in London.

5. Are there any plans to enfranchise? If so, how advanced are these plans? And how much is it likely to cost everybody?

6. What are the service charges?

7. Are there any plans for major works?

8. Is there a sinking fund in place? If so, how much is it?

9. If the lease is shorter than 80 years, can it be extended, and how much would a lease extension cost?

10. Are there any serious debtors in the building?

11. Are there managing agents?

12. Is there a Residents' Association?

13. Is subletting allowed? Under what terms? (This is particularly important to know if you are buying your property as an investment.)

14. Is there a lift?

15. Is there a communal heating and hot water system? Wherever possible, avoid these blocks.

16. Is there a resident porter? Remember, that the more services there are, the more expensive the building is to run, and the higher the service charges.

17. Are all the leases the same? In older buildings, some leases may be different from others. In new buildings, all leases are usually identical. Before buying into an older block, ask if all leases are identical, as having differing leases can cause enfranchisement problems.

Although some of these questions may appear pernickety, it is worth remembering that once you are in, it may be difficult, if not impossible, to change anything. And very often, solicitors do not ask all of these questions. Many conveyancing solicitors, themselves living in secluded mansions in the suburbs, may not understand leasehold law all that well. It is a specialised area, rapidly becoming ever more specialised as laws change and ever more tribunals, regulations and associations start up.

THE LEASE ITSELF

This is usually couched in antiquated legalese and as such, is often not readily comprehensible to the layperson. Because of this, few people buying into leasehold properties ever read the lease or ask to have any clauses they do not understand explained to them.

Then, whenever disputes arise, complainants are first asked to 'refer to the lease' when they may never have even glanced at it before buying into the building.

It is tempting, when documents are written in archaic and unfamiliar language, to imagine they contain some mystic elements beyond the powers of ordinary people to understand. But also, because they seem very stern and legal, there is also the temptation to believe that therefore they must necessarily be fair and above board.

This is by no means always the case. Don't forget that leases are deliberately couched in arcane language to befuddle you, the buyer, and make you think you need a solicitor who charges £200 an hour or more to explain everything. Before buying, always ask to see a copy of the lease; nay, insist on it as once you have signed, it will be too late to undo any clauses you may not like.

If your vendor or solicitor demurs, you can obtain a copy of the lease in any case from the Official Copy Deeds Section of the Land Registry. In recent years, the formerly impenetrable Land Registry has become much more user-friendly and a lot of useful information is obtainable from their website.

THE MAIN ELEMENTS OF A STANDARD LEASE

A typical lease may be 20 or 30 pages long, and it is always written in unpunctuated English. There are no commas, semi colons or full stops. Here is a guide to the main elements of a standard lease:

The current law under which your property is registered to you is the H.M. Land Registry Land Registration Act 2002. This applies even if your lease was issued before this date.

The lease will contain a title number, which is the title number of your property registered with the Land Registry. The property address will then be given, together with the date of the lease, which is the first purchase of the lease and not necessarily *your* purchase.

The particulars will also include details of the lessor, who is your landlord and original lessee. Your property is referred to in the lease as the 'demised property'.

The term 'other demised property' relates to other property included in your lease that you may also own, apart from your actual dwelling, such as a garage, garden shed, garden or outbuildings which are being sold along with the flat.

The term 'premium' refers to the original price paid for the flat. This will be shown in words and figures.

Next will be a series of 'schedules' which set out the terms and conditions under which the lease is granted, and covers obligations on both sides. There will be clauses to say that if you do not pay the ground rent or other money you should pay under the lease or break any of the covenants you have signed for, you may be subject to forfeiture of the lease.

There will also be a reference to service charges. The landlord provides these services, for which you will have to pay a share, usually a percentage set out in the lease. The percentage payable is most often based on the size of your flat, expressed in terms of square metres or square feet. Most often, in modern leases, percentages are expressed per square foot of the property.

The 'Common Parts' referred to in the lease means all those parts of the property not exclusively enjoyed by the lessee, such as stairs, lift, main door and communal gardens.

The lease will have a plan attached which shows the boundaries of your particular property. This is usually outlined in red. There will be a reference to the conduits, pipes and drains which only serve your flat but which may not be situated entirely in your home.

There will also be a paragraph referring to 'internal plastered coverings and other materials on the walls bounding the Demised Premises' (or some such phrase) and this tells you which is your exclusive property and which belongs to the landlord. For instance, windows and window frames are usually the landlord's responsibility although the inside of the frames are your responsibility to maintain.

The whole of the internal walls will be your responsibility including the plaster and any tiles.

There will also be a schedule telling you what rights you have to use other parts of the property such as the entrance hall, lift and stairs. This includes not only yourself but any visitors or workmen coming to your flat.

The lease will contain covenants to ensure that you, the lessee, keep your flat in good condition and are not violating any of the clauses, such as putting in new windows or knocking down internal walls without written permission. In most cases, you cannot carry out major works without the express permission of the landlord, as this may adversely interfere with other parts of the building.

There will also be a clause allowing the landlord or freeholder access to your flat to carry out works or inspections under other clauses in the lease.

FURTHER COVENANTS

These will include the right of the lessee (that's you!) to have sight of the accounts for the previous financial year – usually 1 April to 31 March – and the right of the landlord to charge you in advance for services provided.

There will also be a clause saying that the landlord cannot take automatic possession of your flat for non-payment of service charges but can take court action against you.

Under the terms of the lease, you the lessee agree to pay all utilities not included in the service charges, such as water rates, gas and electricity consumed by you.

On the subject of costs, the lease will also stipulate that you, the lessee, will also have to pay any costs incurred by the landlord for action taken for non-payment of charges. This is always assuming that the landlord is successful in the action.

You will also be required to carry out repairs to ensure your flat is safe, otherwise the landlord can do the work and charge you for it. You can be charged interest on late payments, although the landlord cannot charge interest if there is a dispute, or if more information is needed to determine whether the charges are in fact payable.

You will not be able to put up a television aerial or satellite dish without the landlord's permission, nor will you be allowed to run a commercial business from your flat. You cannot advertise anything from the property either, other than that it is for sale.

There may also be clauses determining what kind of floor covering you are allowed to use, and whether pets are permitted. You will be required, under the terms of the lease, to keep the windows clean inside and out, and have to keep the flat decorated to a 'reasonable' standard. These clauses are very often flouted!

You will not be allowed to play loud music after a certain time, to vacuum carpets before a predetermined time at weekends, or to hang washing out at certain times or in certain places. Nor will building work be allowed after five or at weekends.

LOOK FOR SUBLETTING CLAUSES

Most leases will contain clauses concerning subletting, and in some cases there are restrictions on how you are allowed to sublet. Some landlords require a small deposit if you sublet, and will in any case need to have details of the subtenants, as they may have to be directly contacted on occasion, such as when there is a leak.

There will be many more clauses and obligations than these in most leases, some sounding very arcane, but this is the gist of the typical lease. Most leases follow a standard format, but if there is anything you do not understand, or that seems unclear, check either with your solicitor or, if you baulk at the hourly fees, contact Lease. They are the government's non-profit making leasehold advisory service, who will read and interpret leases for you.

LISTED BUILDINGS

Where the building is listed, buying a flat becomes even more problematic, as in addition to satisfying the landlord or freeholder that you are not infringing any clauses of the lease, you must also abide by listed building regulations.

This can mean you are not allowed to make internal alterations, let alone external alterations, without listed building consent, in addition to any consents you may have to obtain from the landlord or freeholder.

With listed buildings, the local council is concerned to preserve the integrity of the building as much as possible and there will be restrictions on the kind of windows you can have, and the type of external decoration permitted. Very often, you will have to submit architect's plans, which can take months to go through the process.

TIP

Although retrospective planning permission can be obtained, this is a high-risk strategy not to be recommended, as you can be ordered to take down the structure and replace it with the original. It is always better to obtain listed building consent before embarking on any works that might infringe the parameters.

WHERE YOU OWN A SHARE OF THE FREEHOLD

You are still bound by the terms of the lease as you enter into a contract with the limited company, even when you form part of that limited company.

LEASES OF EX-LOCAL AUTHORITY FLATS

These leases will be slightly different from others, in that you may not be able to enfranchise or act as your own managing agents. It may also not be possible to extend the lease of an ex-council flat, particularly in a high-rise block. There will also be clauses relating to how you can sell, at least if you have bought directly from the council as a former tenant at a discount.

Again, make sure you understand all the terms of the lease, as leaseowners in these blocks can often be stung for swingeing charges they did not imagine they would have to meet. If you are in any doubt about any of the clauses in a local authority lease, you can call the relevant Home Ownership Unit for clarification.

TIP

Many councils now provide simplified versions of their leases, and you can obtain a copy on request. It is worth asking for if you are buying an ex-local authority flat. For instance, Hammersmith and Fulham Housing Management Services produce a booklet entitled *Leasehold Ownership: Understanding your lease.* There is not usually a charge for this booklet. Other councils may have similar booklets available on request.

Local councils also provide a yearly rundown of service charges, with a list of what each service costs. Not all private freeholders do this, although accounts are sent to each leaseholder yearly. This is a legal requirement.

EX-LOCAL AUTHORITY BLOCK SERVICE CHARGES

Here is a typical explanation of service charges and how they are allocated, from the Home Ownership Unit of the London Borough of Hammersmith and Fulham.

What am I being charged for?

Those who have bought leases of ex-local authority apartments are charged for: administration, ground rent, insurance, electricity used in the shared areas of the block, security entry systems, lifts and any other equipment that uses electricity.

In addition, annual service charges cover day-to-day repairs and maintenance of the shared areas, caretaking, concierge services, horticulture, water meters, lift servicing and, in tower blocks, booster pumps for ensuring each flat receives fresh water.

These charges are levied every single year and all leaseholders have to pay their share, with five per cent interest over base rate charged for late payments.

Where major works are indicated, these are billed separately once the final account has been settled with the contractor. Beware: these accounts can take years to arrive.

There is a time limit for billing on major works, but local authorities get round this by sending a reminder telling you they have not forgotten about this bill.

PAYMENT PLANS

If you have been charged more than £500 for major works, you may qualify for a loan repayable over a period of years. Most local authorities have a home loans manager who can be contacted at the council offices.

TIP

Unlike many private blocks, ex-council flats are administered by the council's own management team. The 'administration' fee included in yearly service charges is to pay for this management.

Most private blocks do not provide such clear, informative booklets on the whys and wherefores of charges as ex-local authority blocks. The reason for this is that most council blocks contain a mixture of leaseholders who have bought leases, and tenants paying weekly or monthly rent, so it is essential to clarify what leaseholders, but not tenants, must pay. Tenants are not liable for services charges, whereas in a private block everybody is equally liable.

ARE LEASES LEGALLY BINDING?

The answer is 'yes', although in some cases, there may be unfair contracts or unfair terms within them. Also, what is technically legally binding is one thing and what is worth fighting over may well be something else again. Everybody should think very carefully about when and whether it is worth invoking the law, as it is a long, drawn out process where the results may not be what you wished to achieve.

The Leasehold Valuation Tribunal (LVT) publishes a regular bulletin summarising its latest cases, and the reasons for the decisions. In every case, where terms of the lease are disputed, the LVT has ruled that 'the lease is all that matters'.

If a charge is not payable under the lease, it is not payable at all. Similarly, if a charge is payable under the lease it must be paid. And that is the end of the matter. The lease is totally binding on both sides and if ever there is a disagreement, the terms of the lease will be considered absolute and mandatory; as unalterable as the laws of the Medes and Persians.

Who draws up the lease?

It is drawn up by solicitors who copy other leases which is why they are all much the same.

WHAT IF YOU INFRINGE THE LEASE?

Sometimes, this may be done unwittingly but persistent flouting of the clauses of the lease will result in the landlord seeking a court order to repossess the flat. You, the leaseholder, can of course challenge the ruling in an LVT but beware: there is a temptation to imagine the tenant always wins when taking a case to the LVT.

This is by no means always the case. If your behaviour is deemed unreasonable, your lease may be forfeited and you will lose everything.

The ultimate penalty for infringement of the lease is forfeiture, which means that your lease comes to an end and you are thrown out onto the street. In reality, this hardly ever happens.

MAJOR WORKS

All blocks of flats will need major works eventually, and before buying, you need to discover whether these are indicated in the near future. If they have already been agreed, the price of your flat will be reduced by the amount payable by the seller. Never, ever buy a flat with service charges owing. Usually when you buy a flat, there will be service charges paid to beyond the time when you take possession. These will be calculated on a daily basis by your solicitor so that when you obtain possession, you both start with a clean slate.

In some countries, you, the buyer, can find yourself responsible for charges and debts unpaid by the previous owner. In the UK, there are many checks and balances to ensure this does not happen, but whenever you are buying a property with service or other charges unpaid, you need to ensure that you will not become responsible for these. This is something a solicitor should always check.

SERVICE CHARGES

This is one of the most contentious areas of leasehold property, mainly because nobody wants to pay out money and will often try to find any excuse not to pay.

It is usual for the lease to set out what the service charges are and what they cover. Such charges normally cover cleaning of common parts, lift maintenance, rubbish collection, insurance (buildings insurance is a legal requirement) and the cost of the managing agents, if there are any.

There are normally two elements to these charges: service and maintenance. 'Service' typically covers insurance, caretaking, gardening, rubbish collection. 'Maintenance' covers exterior decoration, repointing, replacing pavements or painting the front door or common parts, for example.

You will be billed by the landlord or managing agents for service charges, usually in advance. Most leaseholders pay by standing order, as this is the easiest and quickest method.

These charges may or may not include provision for a sinking or reserve fund, to build up monies for future works. If service charges do not include a sinking fund, they are known as 'interim' charges. One-off levies may in such cases be raised for major works.

The landlord is under an obligation to provide the services set out as charged for in the lease.

REASONABLE CHARGES

Leaseholders are fond of accusing outside landlords or freeholders of profiteering from them. In fact, it is very difficult indeed to profiteer from leaseholders in the modern world. Renske Mann, who became the freeholder of a small block of eight flats in West London, explains:

Many residents don't realise they are paying for services and assume you are ripping them off because they are paying money when it appears they are getting nothing for it. But as with most freeholders, we were a limited company whereby all works had to be supported by bills and you have to be able to produce accounts for all expenditure.

Because you have to produce written proof of all works and expenditure, there is no easy way of making anything out of the building.

What are 'reasonable' charges?

It is said in countless documents that landlords can only collect those charges which are 'reasonable'. The term 'reasonable' does not relate to the amount, only to the fact that the charges can be challenged. Owners can challenge these charges at the LVT, and often do, although they do not always win by any means. It costs a lot more than many people imagine to run a large block of flats.

INSURANCE

It is the freeholder's responsibility to insure the building, usually with a block insurance that comes out of the service charges. There will almost always be an excess to pay for any insurance claim; the amount depends on how many claims the particular block has had in the past. It is usually expected that the excess will come out of the collected service charges; in reality, there may not be enough in the kitty to pay this. The excess on a block insurance policy can easily be £1,000.

ASK FOR EVIDENCE OF EXPENDITURE

The bigger, older or more complex the building, the higher the service charges are likely to be – although this is not always the case, as service charges on brand-new blocks can also be very high, especially where there are such facilities as underground parking, expensive carpets in common parts, landscaped gardens, a swimming pool and gym. As all bills must be supported by receipts, you can always ask to see the accounts, if you are not satisfied as to how the money is being spent. In any case, all residents must be sent a copy of the yearly accounts by the managing agents or whoever is managing the property.

If you are buying a flat, one of the most important questions to ask is whether the service charges are likely to go up in the near future or whether major works are planned. Sometimes, in new buildings, service charges are kept low for a few years and then they rocket.

RECOVERING SERVICE CHARGES

It is very common indeed for disaffected leaseholders to threaten or actually withhold service charges and this causes many problems for all concerned. Some people imagine that paying service charges is optional, and that they can be withheld at will. If enough people do this, then the building goes to rack and ruin and the value of the place plummets.

You are shooting yourself in the foot when you refuse to pay service charges. It is a form of protest which is emphatically not recommended as it means the value of your property goes down. Few people will buy a property if they are told service charges are owing. Also, interest can legally be charged on late payments.

APPLICATION TO THE LEASEHOLD VALUATION TRIBUNAL

If you, either collectively or individually, believe the service charges are too high or 'unreasonable' you can challenge them via the LVT. This is a quasi-legal body whereby three people will sit in judgment at the hearing. Then, your case is either thrown out, or the judgment sent to the County Court for enforcement. If the judgment goes against the landlord or freeholder, they can appeal, and frequently do.

All information regarding the LVT including application forms and scale of costs can be downloaded from the website of the Residential Property Tribunal Service at www.rpts.gov.uk, of which the LVT forms a part.

You as the leaseholder complaining have to complete application form S27A, Landlord and Tenant Act 1985. You then send the completed form with a copy of the lease and details of the service charges under dispute. There is an application fee which varies from £50 to £350 according to the amount in dispute.

The case may be considered either with or without a hearing but even the 'fast track' route is pretty slow, and it will take at least ten weeks for your application to come to the top of the pile.

If the landlord is a large company, they will usually be represented by a Rottweiler-type solicitor who will forcefully argue his client's case. And you should not imagine that the LVT necessarily pronounces in favour of the complainant.

CASE STUDY

Jane and Michael bought a little house attached to a new block of flats, and were billed by the managing agents for their share of the service charges. As their house was completely separate from, although attached to, the main building, with its own front door, and they did not use the lift, common parts or front door of the apartment block, they did not see why they should pay service charges.

The house, they argued, was in the same position as a terraced house in a row and did not share either a roof or foundations with the main block.

Accordingly, they challenged the charges at an LVT hearing, on presentation of all the paperwork demanded. The tribunal took about three minutes to throw the case out and confirm that Jane and Michael were bound by the terms of the lease they had signed. The LVT decided the house was an integral part of the building.

In their case, their percentage of the service charges did not include paying for the lift or cleaning of the common parts, but only for insurance, window cleaning and general maintenance of the exterior.

They went away with their tails between their legs but the cost of the very expensive barrister came out of service charges paid by the other residents. This did not endear them to the rest of the occupants.

The moral of the story is only take your case to the LVT if you have serious grounds for believing your charges to be unreasonable. You need to have direct evidence of this, and not just get the hump because you don't want to pay.

THE LEASEHOLD ADVISORY SERVICE

Lease, the government-funded advisory service, will advise individuals and Residents' Associations on their leases. If you are considering buying a flat and want to check aspects of the lease, this organisation can help. It can also advise on whether certain charges are 'reasonable' and whether they can be legally challenged. But Peter Haler, the founder and Chief Executive, says that if all leaseholders read their lease properly, most of the calls to their office would stop.

The lease is king and this must *always* be remembered when buying a flat. A resident in my building wrote to the managing agents complaining that she objected to some of the terms of the lease. This is tough! She should have had a good look before buying.

Conclusions

There are many complex laws regarding service charges, recovery of these charges and consultations for major works. In reality, landlords – whether outside landlords or where leaseholders own the freehold – will not embark on major works until and unless all the money, or at least most of it, is in.

Local authorities do things the other way round from the private sector: they bill leaseholders after the works have been done and for service charges in arrears. But, then local authorities are a law unto themselves.

Although the government-funded Leasehold Advisory Service states that landlords may not be able to recover costs for major works unless they followed the proper consultation procedure with the leaseholders, most have no money to fall back on anyway and so they cannot carry out the works unless leaseholders agree to them and pay up.

GROUND RENT

This is an annual sum, usually very nominal, for the use of the ground on which the building stands. The payment of ground rent is specified in the lease and is usually included in the service charges. In theory, the landlord or freeholder can instigate forfeiture proceedings for non-payment of ground rent and this in the past has led rogue freeholders to make sure ground rent is not collected, and then start forfeiture proceedings for its non-payment. Such abuses are becoming ever more difficult to sustain.

FORFEITURE AND POSSESSION

This is a stick often waved at recalcitrant leaseholders but it is a last resort and, in reality, very difficult to repossess, as this has to be done by court order. No landlord is allowed just to throw a leaseholder out, however tempting this may be, and however bad their behaviour. The 'innocent until proved guilty' idea is enshrined in our law and applies to late-paying leaseholders just as much as mass murderers. Most of these legal matters take months, if not years, to come to court and by that time the original leaseholder may have sold up and moved on anyway.

Because of the more stringent checks now made by buyers'
solicitors, it is becoming increasingly difficult, if not impossible, to
sell a flat with any outstanding or unpaid charges. It is also
difficult to sell an individual flat where there are service charge
disputes ongoing. Buyers will just run in the opposite direction;
after all, there are plenty of flats on the market which do not have
leaseholder disputes ongoing.

Peter Haler, Chief Executive of Lease advises:

> I cannot say this strongly or often enough: read the lease! Many
> people are not aware when they buy a flat that they have
> entered into a contractual obligation. They don't know what
> they have agreed to when they buy the flat, but half of our
> queries could be solved in advance if buyers only read the lease
> first.

Robert Levene, Chief Executive of the Federation of Private
Residents' Associations, a voluntary body, adds:

> Most people who buy flats have no idea of the terms of the
> lease, and in our view lawyers and estate agents have a lot to
> answer for here.

> When you see a flat and make an offer, the estate agents never
> tell you what the covenants are, and when you get to the
> solicitor stage, they never tell you either. We feel that sight of
> the lease and explanation of its terms should come upfront, not
> when you are about to complete.

> Although the new Home Information Pack has many critics,
> one thing it will do is include a copy of the lease, which all
> prospective buyers should read very carefully beforehand.

Robert Levene says one of the biggest problems concerns pets.

Many, if not most, leases state: no pets, yet buyers keep bringing cats and dogs into the building because they haven't read the lease beforehand. Then they express surprise and say: I didn't know pets weren't allowed. The 'no pets' rule is the one most flagrantly ignored, but eventually the freeholder is likely to seek legal redress for a breach of the lease.

Also, many flat buyers believe service charges are optional. They take the view that they've bought the flat, so why should they keep paying out? But again, service charges will all be on the lease.

COMMONHOLD

Very occasionally, flats may be advertised for sale as 'commonhold'. This type of ownership is common in America, Australia, Cyprus and many other countries, but as yet, rare (and at the time of writing, unknown) in the UK.

It was brought into being by the Commonhold and Leasehold Reform Act of 2002 and came into force in 2004, although leaseholders have yet to take it up. Briefly, commonhold properties are still governed by the lease, as with ordinary leasehold properties, but there is no outside freeholder. Instead, the property – which will usually be a new property – will have been built and developed as a Commonhold property. The lease is known as the Commonhold Community Statement (CCS).

A commonhold is divided into units and common parts in exactly the same way as an ordinary leasehold property, but the difference is that the common parts are owned by the Commonhold Association which has its own title number at Land Registry.

The commonhold association combines the functions of a landlord owning the common parts, a management company providing services and a Residents' Association determining policy and settling disputes.

If a flat you like the look of has commonhold tenure, the Association will be registered at Companies House, and all details will be available from Land Registry. Again, at the time of writing, this is all in the future, mainly because the government has made Commonhold an option, not a necessity.

In my own investigations into newbuilds, either begun or completed in 2005 in the UK, *not one* was a commonhold. All were standard leaseholds, with 99-year leases and an outside freeholder.

But although commonhold seems stretched out into the future, it will happen one day, and it is as well to be prepared.

How does a Commonhold Community Statement differ from a lease?

It will, to all intents and purposes, be exactly the same, except that there is no length of time on the Commonhold Community Statement (CCS) and all units within one block will have an identical document. The provisions of the CCS can be enforced under the terms set out in the document. It is as legally binding as a lease, and there will be dispute resolution procedures set out in the document.

Also, as with a lease, if there are major disputes, the matter can be taken to court. There will be clauses governing how service charges are to be paid, and these are known as the commonhold assessment. Again, as with an ordinary lease, levies can be imposed to pay for unforeseen works and expenses, and assessments can be increased.

A commonhold is a self-managing community but unlike leasehold charges, there is no overriding legal requirement for charges to be 'reasonable'. This means that the charges cannot be challenged at the LVT, or in a court of law.

As a commonhold unit is considered a freehold property, it could be more valuable than a leasehold equivalent. But because commonhold is very new, it is a good idea to take legal advice before proceeding with a purchase if you come across a commonhold unit.

Because commonhold units are not subject to a number of years on a lease, they are not wasting assets. *But* commonhold is new and untried, whereas leaseholds and leases, with all their problems, are at least well-known and familiar. Plus, they are subject to a large amount of statutory regulation. At the time of writing, commonhold units are unregulated by law.

THE MANAGEMENT OF A BLOCK OF FLATS

The following chapter deals with the management of a block of flats, but not everybody understands how this works.

Briefly, if the building is owned by an outside freeholder, they will be responsible for appointing the managing agents.

In some cases, freeholders act as their own managing agents, but in other situations, outside managing agents are appointed to look after the day-to-day running of the building. Where this happens, the leaseholder will have no say in the management of the building, but will just be billed for service and other charges.

Leaseholders can, however, challenge these charges at an LVT if they consider them to be 'unreasonable'. They can also demand to see evidence of expenditure. In any case, managing agents should provide a yearly breakdown of costs to each leaseholder, rather than just presenting them with a total bill.

Where the leaseholders have won the Right to Manage, or have Collectively Enfranchised, they will be responsible for their own management. Again, they can either decide to manage the building themselves, or appoint outside managing agents. There are now firms which specialise entirely in managing blocks of flats and in most cases these will be members of ARMA (the Association of Residential Managing Agents). ARMA was founded in 1991 to put this unregulated business onto a professional footing.

Chapter 4 explains what managing agents do, how to appoint them, and what is involved when management is passed over to a specialist company.

Chapter 5 explains how leaseholders can win the Right to Manage, and wrest management control from outside freeholders or landlords, and also gives information on how to go about Collective Enfranchisement.

New to buying a flat?

If you are new to buying a flat, you need to know about the management of the building. So before making an offer, ask the estate agents:

♦ Does the property have an outside freeholder? (This will normally be the case unless the particulars specifically state 'share of the freehold'.)

♦ If so, who are the managing agents? Does the freeholder use separate managing agents? If so, who are they? And are they members of ARMA? The estate agent will be able to discover these details by going back to the vendor, who must supply answers to these questions.

♦ If the flat you are interested in buying is being sold with a share of the freehold, again ask about the management of the building. Do the residents manage the place themselves, or are there separate managing agents? Again, are they members of ARMA?

This last question is important because ARMA has a grievance procedure you can invoke if you are not satisfied.

TIP

Never buy a flat until you are satisfied you know exactly who owns it, how it is managed, and by whom. Also try to discover, by contacting ARMA, whether the managing agents responsible for looking after the block have a good reputation.

Some buyers who are new to flat living imagine that the managing agents own the building. This is rarely the case, as almost all freeholders will appoint separate managing agents. There is, however, no legal requirement to appoint these agents.

Usually, the managing agents are the hired hands, and act on instructions from the freeholder, or from the Board of Directors where the building has enfranchised.

At the time of writing, around 50 per cent of blocks in Britain have enfranchised, or are in the process of doing so. This percentage is growing all the time, but mainly affects older blocks. Brand-new blocks will almost always *not* be sold with a share of the freehold.

So if you are buying into a newbuild block, you need to know who is going to manage the place.

Management

Another way in which blocks of flats differ from separate houses is that apartment buildings have to be 'managed'.

This means there has to be somebody to collect service charges, prepare accounts, chase up late or non-payers, organise major and minor jobs and generally be responsible for the day-to-day and future smooth running of the building. That same person or company will also have to answer questionnaires when flats are sold, as well as providing three years' worth of accounts and any other information a new buyer might require.

It is a complex job and really needs to be done by somebody who knows what they are doing. Management also has to be undertaken by somebody who is totally trustworthy. If the building has enfranchised, and has therefore become a limited company, accounts have to be filed annually to Companies House, and there must be a Company Secretary.

Where there is an outside freeholder, that person will be responsible for the management of the block and will usually appoint a firm of managing agents, but if the residents have collectively enfranchised or won the Right to Manage, they will either have to manage the building themselves, or appoint their own managing agents.

If the building is owned by an outside freeholder, there may still be a Residents' Association which will hold meetings and discuss affairs to do with the block.

Where a block has not enfranchised or secured Right to Manage, and is happy with the management provided by the freeholder, it may not be sensible to rock the boat. If the residents, in the main, are not happy with the current management, they can take the steps outlined in the following chapter.

Make no mistake, residential block management is complex and time-consuming and nobody should underestimate the work and effort involved.

Many leaseholders do run buildings themselves and, indeed, for several years I was a Director of a block of flats which did undertake its own management. But ask yourself: do you really want to spend every weekend in the office, filling in questionnaires, answering queries, getting plumbers in to mend leaks, collecting money from recalcitrant payers – all for nothing?

Plus if you are in dispute with a neighbour, you are always in danger of meeting that neighbour on the stairs or in the lift. When residents are also undertaking the management there is always the risk of personalising the situation.

Resident management companies

Leaseholders should be aware that if they do have a resident management company this does not mean they can do exactly as they like. Au contraire, as Del Boy might say. A resident management company, even when run by the leaseholders themselves, is subject to exactly the same legal duties as an absentee or commercial landlord.

Duties of managers involve inspecting the physical fabric of the building, and maintaining and decorating it to the right standard. Managers must also have an intimate acquaintance with every aspect of the lease. In addition, those running the building will have to cope with disagreements and personality clashes when they arise. They must also have a thorough knowledge of every aspect of current and future leasehold law.

Maybe the most difficult aspect for resident management companies is dealing with arrears. Whereas a professional managing agent will handle this as part of the job, residents can feel distinctly uncomfortable taking a neighbour to court.

CASE STUDY

When I was helping to run a resident management company, one resident was taken to court for non-payment a total of 47 times. And still we couldn't get any satisfaction as he was too clever for us by half. The stress of going to court and sitting opposite your assailant cannot be underestimated. Indeed, some residents sold up and left because the problems of non-payers, and in particular this non-payer, were causing them sleepless nights.

But as soon as professional managing agents were appointed, those debtors disappeared. Most sold up and left and the rest paid their dues.

ADVANTAGES OF OUTSIDE MANAGEMENT

Where there are six or fewer units in a block, it may be cheaper and easier to manage the building yourselves. When I lived in a block of four flats where everybody owned a share of the freehold, each owner took it in turns to manage the building, and it worked perfectly well.

But with such a small building, there was no caretaker, no lift, and very little day-to-day management required. When major works were indicated, such as when the building developed a severe dry rot problem, we had meetings in each other's flats and raised the money between us. It was all perfectly amicable, but this kind of ad-hoc management would not work in a larger block.

Wherever there are eight or more separate flats, I would say it is imperative to go for outside management, as then the workload becomes too great for amateurs, however well-meaning they are.

Management of buildings containing a number of self-contained units requires proper accounting procedures, an understanding of buildings and how they work. People management skills are useful in that there are often splinter groups within a block – almost always to do with payment of charges and fees.

Where residents run the block themselves, they are usually unpaid and part time. By contrast, a firm of managing agents deals with all the issues that crop up on a full-time basis and employ full-time staff for that sole purpose. Also, they have purpose-bought IT for account handling and they have ready access to lawyers, professional bodies and fidelity insurance cover, none of which individual lessees may be able to match.

Fidelity cover to protect client funds is something that the self-managing lessees cannot probably obtain. Agents also have a separate professional indemnity cover to protect them and again, self-managers might find it difficult to obtain such cover.

The Landlord and Tenant Act 1985

Those managing the building must also be aware of the requirements of the Landlord and Tenant Act 1985, as amended by the Commonhold and Leasehold Reform Act 2002 – regarding 'reasonableness' of costs and formal consultation procedures. It was on such technicalities that we were constantly tripped up by our barrack-room lawyer. Legal documents constituted his bedtime reading, and he constantly sent threatening letters to all the Directors accusing them of malpractice.

Difficult owners

Troublesome residents are less likely to bombard a firm of managing agents with this kind of correspondence, as they are too remote and neutral. I would also say that wherever there are difficult owners, outside management is essential, otherwise it becomes a nightmare living in your own home.

For instance, the landlord must, at the lessee's request, provide summaries of service charge costs, details of insurance requirements and make available for inspection all relevant invoices and documents. Our litigant obtained a court order to photocopy several years' worth of accounts and paperwork, *all at the expense of the company, that is, us.* No wonder there was nothing left over for essential maintenance.

There are many problems you can land yourself with when you attempt to save costs by self-managing. We were constantly being tripped up by our ignorance and niceness. Our litigant kept winning in court by his knowledge and nastiness. The fact that nobody else in the building spoke to him, and most held their noses when passing by him, saying there was suddenly a nasty smell in the air, did not concern him in the least.

He was secure in the knowledge that he was living in the building at everybody else's expense, and revelled in it.

APPOINTING A MANAGING AGENT

The next questions are, how do you appoint good managing agents and how to find them?

In most towns of any size, there will be several firms of managing agents. Sometimes they are dedicated firms or they can be an offshoot of an established estate agency. If you are in the process of appointing new managing agents, contact them and ask for their brochure or prospectus and scale of charges.

Otherwise, log onto the ARMA (Association of Residential Managing Agents) website, where you will find a list of members in your region. Usually their individual websites do not give fees, but they will outline the services they offer.

The next step would be to contact, say, three companies, and ask for a scale of charges and list of services. You, the lessees or representatives of the Company, have to consider which duties you wish to be performed by the agents, and those that you prefer to retain. For instance, you may prefer to go it alone when tendering for major works.

Most managing agents offer a range of services, and you can choose to leave everything to them, or instruct them to take on specific tasks such as collection of service charges. You can decide, for instance, whether the lessees will share cleaning and gardening, or whether the agent should arrange this. Don't forget that every extra service comes at a cost, and this may have to be added on to the existing service charges.

The agents will be directly responsible to the Board of Directors who have full powers of hire and fire, although frequent changes of manager will inevitably disrupt continuity of service provision. It is worth doing some thorough research in advance, rather than chopping and changing agents. When our block was in the process of appointing managing agents, we went through two companies in a few months, before appointing a firm who suited our needs.

The paperwork involved
Never underestimate the sheer amount of paperwork generated when running a block of flats. Any handover from one manager to another takes time and it is quite a complicated procedure.

Lessees who have recently enfranchised and who may not know much about management, can initially ask a surveyor to draw up a formal specification for duties, for discussion with prospective agents.

In any case, you should agree the basic list of tasks before
approaching agents. What do you want to offload and what do
you want to keep for yourself, either to save costs, or because
there are perfectly competent people in the block able and willing
to do certain jobs?

For instance, somebody might agree to take over the garden
because they like gardening. Somebody else might take on the job
of keeping the interior decorated.

What *must* be outsourced when appointing outside agents are the
following: collection of service charges and following up late
payers; responsibility for annual accounts; drawing up tenders for
major works; completing the managing agent's questionnaire
when flats change hands and paying bills to contractors and
suppliers. Usually cheques must be countersigned by an appointed
Director, and this represents a safeguard for the residents.

A typical list of what you might ask an agent
◆ What arrangements are there for general maintenance
  inspections?
◆ How are minor repairs attended to?
◆ How are service charge monies collected?
◆ What are the banking arrangements?
◆ Is there any provision for emergency out of hours call-outs?
◆ What commissions would the agent receive from any contracts?
  All such commissions should be declared in advance.

Standard contracts
The Royal Institution of Chartered Surveyors has produced two
standard contracts; one for purpose-built blocks of flats, and one

for other types of property. The Association of Retirement Housing Managers has a contract especially for retirement housing, as this differs in some important ways from ordinary housing as regards management and service charge payments.

Meetings and qualifications

It is usual for the agent to attend meetings of the Board of Directors, which must be clearly minuted. Most managing agents will attend one or two meetings a year at no extra cost; attendance at others will be billed accordingly. The agent cannot take instructions from individual flat-owners and the position when dealing with requests from individuals must be made clear at the outset.

There are no specific qualifications for managing agents, but membership of appropriate professional bodies is a good start.

TIP
Many professional managing agents will not consider blocks of flats where annual service charges are £1,000 or less.

In blocks that have enfranchised, the usual thing is for the Board of Directors to be responsible for appointing and liaising with managing agents.

Typical charges and services

Below is a list of typical charges and the range of services offered by an ARMA member in 2006:

Initial set-up fee:	£500
Basic management fee:	£150 per annum per unit
ARMA audit of client account:	£250 per annum
Accountancy (outsourced):	£800 per annum
Company secretary duties:	£500 per annum
Commission on major works:	12.5 per cent

In addition, individual lessees would be charged for consent for alterations, unpaid cheques, late payments and completing managing agent's questionnaires when selling.

All of the above fees would be subject to VAT.

THE SET-UP

Where the building has enfranchised, this is the usual arrangement: the Shareholders own the Management Company which appoints the Board of Directors which appoint the Managing Agents who run the management on behalf of the lessees – who are also the Shareholders.

So, as you can see, it is a circular kind of affair where the lessees are also the shareholders who own the management company.

The managing agents do not own the company, as some lessees imagine. They are merely *employees* of the company. But they are given powers by the *Board of Directors* to run the day-to-day affairs of the building.

Where the building has *not* enfranchised, landlords or freeholders may also act as managing agents.

The *agents* have no contract with individual lessees, and their services are limited to those agreed with the Board of Directors and to which a management fee is payable. They will not do any additional work at no extra cost.

It is also the case that any complaints by lessees concerning management must be addressed to the Board of Directors and not to the managing agents.

It is usually the case that individual lessees will contact the managing agents on all sorts of issues, but the agents have no duty to respond unless the request is part of their agreed remit.

All of these are reasons why it pays to appoint managing agents who are members of ARMA, because then any dispute over management can be taken to a higher authority.

WHAT A GOOD MANAGING AGENT WILL DO
I told you it was complicated!

First, the agents must make their fee structure very clear at the outset and also give the Board of Directors a list of other services which may come at extra cost. They cannot just add on costs as they see fit.

In any case, they will agree to manage the client's property in compliance with all applicable legislation. This means they must be aware of any current and future changes in the law. They must be fully conversant with the leases, the Articles of Association (where applicable) and Company Law relating to enfranchised blocks.

The ARMA Code of Practice states that managing agents must provide as cost effective a service as possible. This is obviously a difficult one to quantify, as what constitutes cost effectiveness? All managing agents are plagued by difficult residents, who tend to complain when their lengthy, time-wasting letters are not answered. Ask what their policy is with this type of resident, and whether they charge extra for every letter sent out, over and above the usual correspondence required.

Agents are also responsible for getting quotes for insurance cover, and fully understanding the insurance requirements of the block.

Accounts and funds

So far as money is concerned, agents must ensure that clients' money is kept in a separate, dedicated account and that individual client accounts can be separately identified. This is most important, as funds in one client account must never be used to finance another client's property. The funds must be held in a recognised bank or building society and clearly designated 'Client A/C'.

Cheques must have the block name printed on them, for example 'Fairview Apartments Ltd'. This is so that you know your block has its own separate account.

Any funds or levies raised for major works must be kept in a separate interest-bearing deposit account, away from the day-to-day service charges.

Detailed records must be kept of all transactions and expenditure from the client account suitably authorised.

Agents must also ensure that annual accounting is carried out promptly and be able to supply all paperwork relating to drawing up those accounts which, in the case of a limited company, must be submitted to Companies House by the required date.

Where there is a Residents' Association, managing agents must consult regularly with members. They must also declare an interest in any contractor or business employed to provide services at the property. For instance, if a managing agent also has a construction company, this must be known before the company is invited to tender for works.

TIP

Managing agents are, of course, commercial organisations which exist to make a profit. They will not agree to take on your block unless they can see that it will be cost effective for them. Therefore, it can be difficult to find good managing agents where there are many debtors, if the building is in a terrible state of disrepair, or where there are cliques and factions within the building preventing forward movement.

CODE OF PRACTICE

All managing agents who are members of ARMA will have a Code of Practice, which can be given to the Residents' Association on request. It should be noted that the profession, if you call it such, of managing agents is unregulated, and there is no requirement for them to become members of ARMA. This does not mean they are no good, but there may not be a grievance procedure, or any higher authority to whom to appeal if things go wrong.

As ever more blocks enfranchise or gain the Right to Manage, it is important to appoint a thoroughly professional company to manage the property, especially as the likelihood is that residents themselves will not know much about running the block.

Please also note that any managing agent, however conscientious or reliable, is just doing a job. The building is not their home and as such, they are never going to take as much interest in it as you do.

To me, the most important aspect of appointing managing agents is that they take all the emotion out of running a block of flats. They should be calm, detached and professional, whereas when leaseholders run their own block, emotions tend to run very high.

FORMING A RESIDENTS' ASSOCIATION

Where the block has not enfranchised, it is always worth forming a properly-constituted Residents' Association.

Where it has enfranchised, leaseholders will be members and shareholders of the company, so there is probably not a lot of point in adding another layer, as the whole purpose of the Residents' Association is to form a collective voice when it comes to spending money and keeping up the standard of the block.

A brief outline of Residents' Associations' purposes

Detailed information can be obtained from the Federation of Private Residents' Associations, but here is a brief outline of the function and purpose of such Associations.

- They can make the landlord or agent carry out regular inspections, and have a say in the expenditure of their own money.

- They can meet the landlord or agent to discuss the needs of the residents and negotiate with either residents or landlords and assist in resolving disputes between residents.

- They can apply for a determination of the reasonableness of service charges (most important) and make sure they are consulted on major works.

It is often useful to form a Residents' Association in advance of trying to obtain collective enfranchisement. In any case, it makes sense for any lessees who have an outside landlord to form an Association. This can be exercised in both the private and public housing sectors, but there is, as always, a right and wrong way to form such an Association.

First, all residents have to be circulated, excluding the landlord and any employees such as a caretaker, with a letter giving a brief history of the block and a tear-off form to be sent back to the organiser. It is a good idea to include a stamped addressed envelope, as nowadays it seems it is too much trouble for many people to buy an envelope and a stamp and find a letter box.

Ask some supporters to form an Acting Committee. One person should also be designated an Acting Chairperson. Then call an informal meeting of the residents, explaining what the proposed new Association is all about.

The best way of setting up an Association
At an early stage, contact the FPRA (Federation of Private Residents' Association), a non-profit making body, which will

advise on the best ways of setting up such an Association. There will have to be an annual subscription, and when the group is up and running, an Honorary Secretary has to be appointed, who is responsible for taking minutes and keeping records. There will also be a subscription charge to the FPRA, and a charge for their very useful booklets and instruction manuals.

After the initial meeting, the new Association should apply to the landlord for recognition. Again, the FPRA can help out here, as you will need a Constitution, which can be quite lengthy and involved, but which is necessary if the Association is to be properly run.

Once the Association is formed, with a Chairman, Secretary and Committee, meetings must be held. These usually consist of an AGM (Annual General Meeting) and possibly a number of EGMs (Extraordinary General Meetings), to discuss more urgent issues that cannot wait for the AGM. With EGMs, the same procedure has to be followed as for an AGM.

TIP

When I belonged to a Residents' Association, the only formal meeting was the AGM. Otherwise, there were social meetings, Christmas parties and other such events, which all helped to bind the residents together. There is not always something to complain about, but even when everything runs smoothly, it is still a good idea to have an Association.

Outside landlords and recognised Residents' Associations
It is *always* a good idea to have a Residents' Association in a

block of flats where there is an outside landlord. And such Associations can have legal force, as they may seek statutory recognition from the landlord. Again, the FPRA can help here with its explanatory pack. Recognised Residents' Associations have more power than informal ones and they are entitled to be consulted about the appointment of managing agents; be notified of works proposed by the landlord and receive a copy of estimates; submit the names of alternative contractors; obtain information about service charge accounts and appoint their own surveyor.

Where it might be too difficult to enfranchise or go for Right to Manage, a recognised Residents' Association may be the next best thing. It is easier than the other options and, in many cases, can work just as well.

Robert Levene, Chief Executive of the FPRA, explains further:

> We advise our members on all issues relating to living in a flat and also lobby governments and make representations on legislation.

> The biggest issue is always payment of service charges as many flat owners believe these are optional. One reason for this is that few solicitors or estate agents ever point out what the covenants are and how they are enforced. Very many people buy flats believing they don't have to pay Service Charges if they don't want to. We are hopeful that the new Home Information Pack will change this attitude.

Most managing agents, he adds, don't themselves live in flats – because they know only too well what the problems are.

WHERE YOU HAVE ENFRANCHISED

All residents in possession of a membership certificate – given to you when you buy the property – are members of the Company and as such will be invited to attend the AGM. Although attendance at AGMs is not required, it is compulsory to hold such a meeting, which will be chaired by the Chairman and the Company Secretary will take the minutes.

The AGM will consist of approval of accounts, the Chairperson's report, updates on debtors, reports on major and minor works and any other changes since the last year and, finally, Any Other Business – which is usually where the fun starts. It is the Chairperson's job to keep order – and a firm hand will often be required.

There may be matters on which members may vote, such as the appointment of new managing agents, a new Chairperson or new Directors and the usual thing is, one vote per flat. This means that if one person owns three flats, they get three votes, but if four people live in one flat, they only get one vote between them.

Debtors or those in arrears may attend the meeting but will not be allowed to vote. Friends or relatives of members may be allowed to attend the AGM (should they wish to) but must remain silent. They are not allowed to offer opinions and comments, or to vote.

There may also be one or two Extraordinary General Meetings (EGMs) throughout the year, such as when emergency major works are indicated, and cannot proceed without a majority vote from members.

AGMS and EGMs must be minuted, which does not mean that everything has to be taken down verbatim. The gist of what was said is good enough, although it must be accurate.

Occasionally, there may also be Directors' meetings and these must also be minuted. The managing agents will usually attend these meetings, but there may be an extra fee for such attendance.

These are the formal aspects of management. But the main aim in a block of flats is to make sure everybody gets along – and this is often more difficult to achieve than the formal aspects.

5

Increasing the Value of Your Flat

Most people hope that when they buy property its value will go up.

Unfortunately, when you buy a flat, or indeed any leasehold property, its value can go *down* instead as the years go by and the lease gets ever shorter. Indeed, if the length of the lease is edging dangerously near to 80 years, the value of the flat will rapidly decrease.

In the old days, this was a severe drawback to leasehold homes, and meant that anybody who had a choice, bought freehold properties instead.

Another serious drawback to buying leasehold flats was the often difficult relationship with the freeholder. Although all leases state that the freeholder has a duty to keep the property in good condition, this clause was frequently broken by freeholders who could no longer afford to maintain the building, who could not be bothered, who simply disappeared and went away or waited for leases to run down so that they would own the building again.

These factors are the main reasons why, eventually, even originally valuable flats lost a lot of value. It is still quite common to find leases of 54 years or less on older blocks, and the long-term residents have no idea their property is worth virtually nothing until they come to try to sell.

But where the lease is less than 80 years, you cannot sell your flat – or at least, only for a knockdown price to a cash buyer.

But fear not! There are now three ways of increasing the value of your property, even when the lease is getting short, the common parts are run down and the freeholder has absconded or completely lost interest in the building.

The options are:
1. You can extend your lease by 90 years.
2. You can exercise your right to manage.
3. You can buy the freehold by a process known as collective enfranchisement (CE).

All these are options you can *force* your landlord or freeholder into doing. There are exceptions for some kinds of property, but in the main, anybody who lives in a leasehold property can exercise one or all of these steps, which increase the amount of control you have over your own property.

But although you can extend your own lease individually and without reference to the other residents, in order to buy the freehold or exercise the right to manage, you need to take collective action, and get a majority of residents on your side. This is not always easy, especially as collective enfranchisement can cost each leaseholder a lot of money which, they feel, may not be realised in extra value on the flat.

There is also a common attitude among older residents that the lease, however short, will 'see them out' and they may not want to spend their remaining savings on something that may only benefit their heirs or, more likely these days, the taxman.

Where this is the case, it may not be possible to get enough support to enfranchise, and extending your lease may be the only answer.

WHAT YOU NEED TO KNOW BEFORE YOU BUY

Whenever considering buying a leasehold property, first look at the length of the lease on the agent's particulars. If this information is not there, as is often the case, ask before going any further with the purchase. When the lease is 80 years or less, ask whether this term can be extended, and about how much it would cost. Very often estate agents fudge the length of the lease by putting something like 'lease 125 years from 1986' or something, which may lull you into a false sense of security.

Although buyers can now legally force the freeholder to grant them a 90-year lease extension on most types of leasehold properties, not all leases can be extended. Specialist properties such as those held on crown leases, National Trust properties, and those within cathedral precincts are exempt from this legislation. But, in practice, few people are likely to live in these apartments.

In any case, freeholders of these properties have expressed a desire to go with the prevailing legislation, which means that in practice, crown leases, for instance, often can be extended. So, if you are considering buying one of these 'exempt' properties, find out what the leasehold/freehold/lease extension situation is before buying.

The procedure

For most other privately-owned buildings, all or any of the above three options can be exercised, although there is a standard procedure which must be followed in each case. For instance, even if you want to extend the lease, you would normally have to wait two years after buying before doing so. You would not be able to extend the lease before buying, but if you know that it can be extended, and what it is likely to cost, this knowledge can form part of your negotiations on the asking price of the property.

If you have fallen in love with a particular flat, but the leasehold arrangements leave much to be desired, what do the various value-increasing options have to offer and what do they entail?

EXTENDING THE LEASE

This is in many ways the easiest option to exercise, as you can do it on your own without involving any of the other residents; all other options need the consent of at least 50 per cent of owners to proceed.

A lease of less than 80 years is a fast-wasting asset, mainly because few mortgage companies will advance loans. This makes the property difficult to re-sell. So if you are interested in buying an apparently bargain-price flat with a short lease, check first that (a) the lease is theoretically extendable and (b) that it will not cost you a punitively high sum. In general, the shorter the lease, the more it costs to extend.

In some instances, the lease extension process has started, but not been completed, when a flat goes on the market. In this case, the seller can transfer the right to the lease extension to the buyer.

Although you can legally extend a lease these days by 90 years, freeholders can drive a ridiculously hard bargain, so do not imagine it will always be a simple option.

The relevant legislation states that the lease extension must be bought at the current market price – don't imagine you will get it for nothing, or nearly nothing, because you are already living there. Also, working out the numbers can be horrendously complicated.

CASE STUDY

Eileen, a retired doctor in her 70s, had just 16 years left on the lease of her home in London, W1. Although the lease would probably see her out, she wanted to have something to leave her children, and so applied to the freeholders, Howard de Walden Estates, for a 90-year extension as was her legal right.

They agreed, but valued it at a whacking £700,000. Eileen felt the lease extension was worth about half of that, and took her case to the LVT after getting the place professionally valued, itemising all the improvements she had made over the years, and getting all the other necessary paperwork in place.

The freeholders vigorously contested this and would not back down, arguing that this was what a 90 year lease on this particular property was worth on the open market. A fierce battle, not to say a stressfully long two-year wait, ensued and the upshot was that Eileen lost her case as the LVT ruled that the extension was, in fact, worth £700,000 on the open market. The improvements she had carried out did not, they decided, significantly add to the value as the property was worth more or less the same whatever its condition, simply because of its very central location. Legal fees came to over £8,000.

TIP

Improvements made to a leasehold property by the leaseholder do not necessarily increase its value; it is the length of the lease which is the determining factor.

The moral of the above story is: if you do not accept the price the freeholder states for your lease extension, be prepared for an almighty battle that you may lose.

In general though, if the case does go to the LVT, they will usually rule that the lease extension is worth something between the valuation put it on it by the freeholder (selling) and the leaseholder (buying).

Here is the outcome of a more typical situation

Length of lease:	62 years
Lessee's valuation:	£4,000
Landlord's valuation:	£8,500
LVT valuation:	£5,170

Existing value:	£140,000
Extended value:	£150,000
Ground rent:	£12.60 pa
'Marriage value':	£9,661

'Marriage' value

The term 'marriage value' describes the extra value created by 'marrying up' the leasehold and freehold elements or, in this case, the difference between the value of the property with the short lease and the extended lease. The term 'marriage value' is one you have to constantly keep in mind when extending leases or buying the freehold. The shorter the lease, the higher the marriage value.

For instance, a flat with 62 years left on the lease is valued at £140,000 on the open market. With a 90-year lease extension, it is valued at £150,000. Therefore, the 'marriage value' is £10,000.

The term 'marriage value' does not apply where the lease has 80 or more years to run. For the purposes of negotiation, an 85-year lease is as valuable as a 999-year lease.

Lease extensions

Although you do not buy the freehold when extending a lease, you will certainly increase the value of the flat when it comes to selling, and sometimes going it alone is the easier option. It can be difficult persuading the other leaseholders to join forces with you.

The cost of a lease extension mainly depends on how tough a bargain the freeholder wants to drive, although offers on both sides must be supported by hard evidence, and not just be figures plucked out of the air. If the freeholder is prepared to extend the lease for nothing, or nearly nothing (which sometimes happens) there will be no need to take the case to the LVT. Likewise, if you can agree a figure between you, there will be no need to take the case to the LVT.

Nowadays, though, there are few ways the freeholder can make money out of the lessees, and selling lease extensions can be highly profitable, so don't be surprised if your freeholder rubs his hands together and demands a large amount when you apply to extend the lease.

A typical example

A one-bedroom flat was on the market for £155,000, with a 63-year lease. In this case, the lease could be extended by 90 years, at a cost of £10,000. The price is non-negotiable, according to the freeholder.

In my view, it would be well worth paying the extra £10,000, as the lease had become too short for the value of the property to be maintained.

With the 90-year extension, making a total lease length of 153 years, the flat would rise in value in accordance with the market.

THE PROCESS

The relevant legislation here is Chapter 11 of the Leasehold Reform Housing and Urban Development Act. Assuming you qualify for a lease extension, the first thing is to get the property professionally valued. This valuation does not just assess the resale value of the property but also the loss to the freeholder, as he will not get the flat back as quickly as he had hoped. Thus, it would cost considerably more to extend a lease with 16 years remaining, than one with 80 years remaining.

The valuer will do all the necessary sums, which can be quite complicated, as the valuation of the freeholder's interest has to be calculated as well.

This valuation is based on the rental income, i.e. ground rent for however many years, the reversion (the eventual vacant possession of the property) and any other parts that may be included, such as a garage, outbuilding, garden or roof terrace.

Expert leasehold valuer Stewart Gray, of the firm Austin Gray says:

> It is very important to obtain expert guidance on valuation, as any missed information will automatically invalidate the notice.

> Because the implications for short leases are now very serious, anybody contemplating selling their flat should get the lease extended before they sell.

But if you are desperate to buy a flat which has a worryingly short lease, the fact that you are legally allowed to extend the lease (apart from those properties excluded from the legislation) may give some comfort.

Another example of a typical set of figures for a lease extension

A flat where the leaseholder sought to extend the lease had 48 years remaining. The value put on this flat with its short lease was

£116,000. The value after lease extension was calculated at £145,000, making an uplift in value of 24.5 per cent. The premium paid by the leaseholder for the extension was £16,800, and the case did not go to the LVT as there was no dispute over the figures.

If there is no dispute and the matter proceeds smoothly, a lease extension should take seven or eight months to complete. Where the amounts are disputed, it could take more than a year, with fees building up all the time.

Before embarking on a lease extension, check what the professional fees are likely to be as, of course, these will be in addition to the cost of the lease extension itself.

TIP

There are some companies nowadays which specialise in project managing lease extensions and collective enfranchisement. These companies will oversee every aspect including valuation and legal work, for a flat fee. See Resources (page 208) for a list. Also, lease extensions are by definition individual affairs, and will not extend to the entire block. If your block is in the process of enfranchising, the landlord is not allowed to sell you a lease extension as well. Anyway, there would be no point, as once you have enfranchised, leases can be extended for nominal sums.

GETTING STARTED

The first thing is to get the flat valued, at both its present value and at its new value with the lease extension. For this you will need an estate agent or a chartered surveyor; it is not enough to just guess the old and new values, although valuations are not an exact science and there will always be some degree of guesswork. These papers should be presented to your solicitor, who will serve the requisite Section 41 notice on the landlord.

If you do not know who the freeholder is, and these days it is not always easy as freeholds can change hands very quickly, you must find out before the notices can be served. This information is now available at www.landregisteronline.gov.uk. If your building has managing agents, they will more than likely have details of the freeholder or overall owner. Your solicitor will also need a copy of your original lease.

Your solicitor then has to convey your offer price to the freeholder, who will probably come back with a counter (higher) offer price. The landlord has to reply to the notice within two months, and he can also inspect the flat in this time, to carry out his own valuation of the place.

If the landlord does not come back within the statutory time, the lessee can buy the lease extension at the original offer price by applying to the County Court for a 'vesting order'.

However, don't bank on the landlord forgetting all about it and missing the deadline! In reality this hardly ever happens, as selling lease extensions is a lucrative business.

The landlord's response
The next step is that the landlord, or his representative on earth, will respond, usually with a (higher) counter offer. There will very

likely also be a demand for a deposit of, typically, £250, from you to show that you are serious.

Unless the landlord and lessee can reach agreement on the amounts, one or other party will have to apply to the LVT. This will normally be done by the leaseholder's solicitor and is another reason why it is important to instruct a solicitor fully conversant with the process.

If agreement cannot be reached
The LVT hearing is held, usually three to four months after receiving the application. There will be three people on the LVT panel, such as a lawyer, surveyor and layperson. The leaseholder can be present at the hearing, and I would advise it, but this is not a legal requirement and you can be represented by your solicitor.

If your landlord is a large corporation, it will almost always be represented by a fierce solicitor used to this kind of thing. The LVT panel will listen carefully to both sides, then go away to assess all the evidence and pronounce, sending details of its decision to each side.

If the lessee finds the eventual price too high, he can walk away from the deal and not pursue the request for a lease extension. The landlord can also appeal if he considers the price too low. In either case, the appeal must be lodged within 28 days of the original decision and it will now be heard by the Lands Tribunal.

If the landlord believes the lessee's offer is ridiculously low, he can apply to the County Court to have the notice declared invalid.

This will have the effect of stopping the lease extension process for at least another year.

So, you can see how the business can drag on and on when parties cannot reach agreement. And every extra letter, phone call, email or fax means a fatter fee for the lawyers.

It's done!

Assuming agreement is reached, either privately or at the LVT, the term of the extension is entered on the lease and the money paid by the lessee.

How long does it all take?

If the valuation put on the lease extension is challenged by the landlord at the LVT, you are looking at a timeframe of at least a year, by which time values could have changed.

How much does it cost?

This is where it pays to do your sums very carefully indeed, before proceeding with an extension. There are several cost elements, such as the cost of the lease extension itself; the solicitor's and surveyor's costs – payable whether or not the application succeeds – and the landlord's solicitor and surveyor fees. In general, it costs about the same to extend the lease as to enfranchise collectively. Legal and other fees alone could easily come to £3–4,000.

There is no application fee to the LVT, and if the case proceeds to an LVT hearing, each side pays its own costs. Because many landlords hate paying out, most lease extensions are concluded before getting to the LVT stage. As ever, it depends on how much money is involved. In Eileen's case on page 108, the sum was so large that it was worth the landlord's while to pay legal costs for an LVT hearing.

WHICH IS BETTER, A LEASE EXTENSION OR COLLECTIVE ENFRANCHISEMENT?

Collective enfranchisement is definitely the better option. Most experts advise that, wherever you can, it is better to enfranchise collectively than just extend your own lease. Flats which come with a share of the freehold are always more valuable than even the longest lease.

Why is this?

Because it means that there is no outside freeholder to impose control. Not only that, but there is a uniformity about the building. If you have extended your lease to, say, 138 years, yet all the other flats in the building have leases of 48 years, you will be a high-value flat surrounded by low-value flats in the same building.

Also, once the building has collectively enfranchised, there is nobody making any money out of the leaseholders, and leases can be extended very cheaply.

CASE STUDY

Jim and Carol bought a very cheap flat with a 70-year lease, which was worrying, but the building, containing 33 flats, had just enfranchised and formed a limited company. The couple paid £33,000 in 1999 for the flat.

After a couple of years, they applied to extend their lease to 999 years, and this cost just £750, plus costs to the Land Registry to alter the title deeds and solicitors' fees, in total another £100.

Jim and Carol had paid cash for their flat, but wanted the extension because it would be difficult to resell except to a cash buyer, with such a short lease.

After extending the lease, the flat's value increased to £115,000 overnight.

VERY SHORT LEASES

Where the leases on all the flats in a building have become very short, say 30 years or less, check whether it is actually worth trying to extend or enfranchise. I once received particulars on a property with only a 35-year lease left. The reason the leases were running down was that the building was not expected to last much longer, and was scheduled to be pulled down when the leases finally ran out.

Because the building was right on the seafront, with a fabulous view, I would have secured a wonderful location at a very cheap price – but only for a certain length of time. I decided not to buy, but in some instances it could still be worth it if you regard the lease as a cheap and never-increasing rent for the remaining life of the building.

It is possible, in this case, that the land on which the building stands will eventually be more valuable than the actual units. But 35 years is a long time to wait to find out.

RIGHT TO MANAGE

All blocks of flats have to be managed by somebody, and it is very common for individual lessees to moan continuously about the inferior way the building is managed, and how everybody is being overcharged for very poor services.

The Commonhold and Leasehold Reform Act of 2002 allows leaseholders to take over the management of their building, even when it is owned by an outside freeholder, and without having to prove any dereliction on the part of the landlord.

In fact, lessees have not been overwhelmingly keen to take over the management themselves where there is an outside freeholder, maybe because managing a block of flats is quite hard work, and requires a level of expertise that residents may not possess. It is quite a big responsibility, especially when residents are managing the building voluntarily.

Also, setting up a Right to Manage (RTM) company is complicated in itself, and you have to get at least half the owners agreeing before it can be taken any further. It is not always easy to overcome apathy. Reluctant residents have to be persuaded that services will become both better and cheaper when the flat owners are in charge – and they may not be convinced that this will necessarily happen.

In some cases though, gaining RTM may be a first step towards collective enfranchisement, especially if the landlord is trying to charge a huge amount to let go of the freehold to the residents. But before ever deciding on this step, it is essential for interested residents to read the lease very carefully, and ensure they can fulfil all its provisions themselves.

Once the residents gain an RTM, there is really no way the landlord can continue to make money out of them, except by selling them the freehold.

HOW TO GO ABOUT SETTING UP AN RTM

So long as the building itself qualifies – and again, local authority and many housing association properties are not included – an RTM company may be set up and registered with Companies House. This is a company limited by guarantee, and means that the RTM must keep proper accounts which are submitted to Companies House every year, and anybody is entitled to look up the company. The RTM must also have a Memorandum and Articles of Association – you can get copies of the MemArts, as it is called, from the Stationery Office.

In fact, it is relatively easy to set up a limited company, as all the rules and regulations are in place, and the Companies House website will guide you through it. But once the company has been set up, you have to abide by Company law. The fact that the RTM is non-profit making, and just run by residents, does not mean it escapes the strictures. For instance, the company must hold an AGM, appoint directors and submit proper accounts every year. Otherwise, the company can be struck off, even though it is not trading in any way.

You cannot just make it all up as you go along!

When trying to set up an RTM, all residents must be invited to become members, and sent the right forms, even if you may not want some occupants to be included. You are not allowed to exclude any of them, even known troublemakers. Then, once at least 50 per cent of the flats become members, the RTM company is deemed to be set up, and can apply for RTM.

After this, the landlord is sent an RTM claim notice and has a minimum of one month to reply. He may decide to serve a counter-notice on the RTM company, either admitting their right to manage, or disputing such. If he does not send a counter-notice, the RTM company can begin managing without further ado.

Otherwise, the LVT is involved – again. If the RTM claim is disputed, the company applies to the LVT, which makes a decision as to whether the RTM notice is valid and whether the RTM company actually has the right to take over the management.

Assuming the LVT upholds the RTM decision, the landlord can then become a member, if desired. In any case, he must provide the RTM company with a list of all contractors and any other matters concerning the management of the building such as lift operators, maintenance people, fire safety regulations and insurance.

The RTM is not bound to continue using the same contractors or service providers.

How long does setting up the RTM take?

Even if everything proceeds smoothly, it will still take about a year from start to finish. The shortest timescale is probably eight or nine months, so it cannot just be a decision by a few disgruntled residents objecting to what they have to pay.

It also costs something to set up an RTM, to register with Companies House and comply with the strictures of the Companies Act. The new company must also bear the costs of the landlord in handing over or disputing the claim although should the case proceed to the LVT, each side will pay its own costs, unless the LVT decides the RTM is not eligible, when it will have to pay the costs of the other side as well.

Setting up an RTM is not something to be entered into lightly, then!

Also, establishing an RTM does not mean that the residents now own the block. Unless they have also collectively enfranchised, the landlord can sell on the freehold to somebody else, although where an RTM exists, he must offer the residents the right of first refusal.

What the RTM has to do

Once set up, the RTM is responsible for carrying out all the provisions of the lease such as insurance, cleaning, renovations, day-to-day repairs and major works.

Is it better for residents, having gained RTM, to manage the building themselves, or go for outside management?

On balance, it is probably better to go for professional management in a building of any size. However, specific management issues are discussed in the following chapter.

Be aware of the problems associated with RTMs

RTMs may sound a good idea but be warned. They do not always work smoothly by any means. This is because an overwhelming problem with a block of flats is that it is rare for all to think alike, and it is common for residents to squabble among themselves after gaining RTM. I would emphatically not recommend going for RTM where there are already disputes and disagreements among residents. You need a sense of community, for all to think as one, for RTM to work. If there are warring factions, as there frequently are, it may be better to stick with the existing management structure.

Because residents can demand to see accounts, it is becoming increasingly difficult for freeholders to rip off residents through service charges, levies and other fees. Also, residents often do not realise just how much it costs to run a building satisfactorily; insurance alone can take up half the annual charges.

In fact, RTM is not proving as popular as expected, possibly because the whole thing involves quite a lot of work and you don't even own your building at the end of it.

Peter Haler, chief executive of LEASE, the government's leasehold advisory service, has this to say about RTMs:

> Over the past few years, there has been a drastic decline in enquiries about RTM and it's hard to understand why. Only six

per cent of enquiries to LEASE are about RTM, yet to us at
LEASE it is often the answer. It does not cost anything, unlike
extending your lease or collective enfranchisement, and given
that concern about quality of management and level of service
charges is the commonest reason for wanting to buy the
freehold, one would expect us to be deluged with enquiries.

As it gives the leaseholders the management, it would seem the
obvious way to improve your building.

LEASE provides free legal advice to leaseholders, landlords,
managers and anybody else connected with issues affecting
residential leasehold properties.

Many firms of managing agents also now handle RTMs. A list
can be obtained by logging onto the ARMA website
www.arma.org.uk. Individual entries by members will indicate
whether or not they handle setting up an RTM.

BUYING THE FREEHOLD, OR, COLLECTIVE ENFRANCHISEMENT

There is no doubt that this is by far the best option, if you can get
enough residents to agree and if you qualify. Most importantly,
ensure you can all afford it, as buying the freehold can be
expensive in itself, not to mention the legal and professional costs
involved, even when the whole thing goes smoothly – which it
rarely does.

In practice, most residential blocks of flats where occupants have
leases in excess of 21 years remaining will qualify for CE
(collective enfranchisement). But there must be at least 50 per cent
of the leaseholders (not subtenants, but long leaseholders) who

agree in principal to the enfranchisement.

Why enfranchise?

The reasons are obvious: you, the residents, gain control and ownership of the building, which then belongs to a company you have created and in which you all have a share. This means you can decide on policy, appoint managing agents or manage the building yourselves, decide on service charge rates, major and minor works, appoint your own contractors and generally, not be beholden to the freeholder any more.

The trouble is, many residents talk about enfranchising when they are dissatisfied with the existing structure, or service charge payments. Kat Callo, whose company Rosetta Consulting, specialises in collective enfranchisement, advises:

> It is very important for residents to move forward rather than fight yesterday's battles.

> They are over. When enfranchising, you have to put your emotions, and any feelings of revenge or anger, to one side and proceed in a positive direction. Collective enfranchisement is a complicated procedure with many ways of being tripped up. To make it work, you need all your focus and resources in one place.

MAKING IT WORK

Each participant *must* at an early stage sign a Participation Agreement. This is not required by law but binds you all together at the beginning of negotiations, and also ensures some commitment from those interested. Unless this is done, you find that people start changing their minds and you get nowhere.

After agreement is reached, and enfranchisement is theoretically possible – and this will usually depend on the hard work of the one or two people pushing the agreement forward – a Right to Enfranchise Company has to be set up. This is, like the Right to Manage company, a Company Limited by Guarantee, which must be registered at Companies House.

After the Company has been set up, each participant will be a shareholder in the new company. Non-participants are not shareholders. Obviously, each participant has to advance some money, which should be put in a separate, dedicated, account, as there will be costs at the outset, and ongoing costs as the matter proceeds. It is not cheap to enfranchise.

Gaining a formal valuation

The next step is to get a formal valuation of each flat within the building. The building itself minus the flats is worth nothing, but that does not mean there is no value to the freeholder. Depending on the length of the lease, the main value may be in the reversion, which is when the property reverts to the landlord. And the shorter the lease, the higher the reversion value.

Ground rent

There is also value in the ground rents, and to arrive at this, the surveyor will have to add up the total price paid in ground rents over the years the leases still have left to run. A simple example would be: in a block of 100 flats, each leaseholder pays £100 a year in ground rent, and the leases have 70 years to run. Assuming no increase, the total ground rent comes to £700,000 over that 70 years. Now you can start to see how small sums add up, and why collective enfranchisement is rarely simple.

Valuation of the enfranchisement

Where there is a marriage value, which there will be when leases are less than 80 years, the freeholder's share is set at 50 per cent of this. Where the leases all have more than 80 years to run, the marriage value does not apply.

A lease of 80 years is considered as valuable as one of 125 years; there is no difference in purchase price when flats are sold on after enfranchisement. The 'share of the freehold' is the magic term which automatically increases the value of the flat.

The valuation is made up of each leaseholder's interest (the value of each flat on the open market, now and after enfranchisement) and the freeholder's interest. In other words, by buying the freehold, how are you depriving the freeholder?

Appreciation

There is also the expected appreciation in value once the freehold is bought, to take into account.

Some buildings may have garages, outbuildings, communal gardens. There may be some flats over shops, and also the freeholder may own some flats which are rented out on a monthly basis. There may be a caretaker's flat or there may be a head leaseholder, who comes halfway between the landlord and the leaseholders. This happens in many blocks of flats in prime Central London, such as Belgravia and Knightsbridge. In all, there are many variables, and all have to be taken into account when totting up the value of the building as no two blocks of flats are exactly alike.

The right of first refusal

There may also be the 'right of first refusal' to consider. Many freeholders sell on their interest to other freeholders, and there is much exchange of this kind in the property market. When this happens, they must now by law offer the freehold to the leaseholders first, at the same price. This happens mainly with new blocks, where developers own the freehold for a few years, then move on.

'Hope' value

In addition, there may be 'hope' value, where the freeholder hopes to build a couple of storeys on top, for instance, or development value, where there is spare land owned by the freeholder on which he intends to build. When Marion Mathews and Renske Mann sold the freehold of their building in London, W11, they retained 'air rights' which means they can, if they should ever want to, build another storey on top of the existing building.

Solicitors conversant with CE should know all about possible future development value.

Summary

To sum up, there are three main elements to the valuation: the landlord's interest, such as income stream from future ground rents; the landlord's interest – the value of the reversion, when he gets the properties back and the MV of participating flats, where this is payable.

As with lease extensions, MV does not apply where the leases have 80 plus years to run. Where leases have less than this time to run, the leaseholders pay 50 per cent of the marriage value to the freeholder.

Example: each flat is currently worth £500,000, with a 70-year lease left. After enfranchisement, each flat would be worth £600,000. The marriage value is therefore £100,000, of which participating enfranchisers would pay £50,000 each.

How it stacks up (sample)
Here is a sample valuation for each flat valued at £580,000 with a 60-year lease and ground rent payable at £200 pa. The estimated freehold value of this same flat is £700,000.

Ground rent: total value	£5,470
Reversion	£28,140
MV	£43,195
Cost of freehold per flat:	£76,805

This means that each participant pays £77,000 to get £700,000 value.

But there is more to it than that, because a flat sold with a share of the freehold is *always* more valuable than the same flat sold without this advantage. Also, such a property would rise in value according to the market, whereas with a 60-year lease remaining, it would only lose value.

(Figures courtesy of Rosetta Consulting.)

CASE STUDY

In 1999, Colin bought a newbuild property in a block of 13 flats on the Sussex coast. By the time the development was finished, the developer had gone bust. He offered the freehold to the residents who could not reach agreement to enfranchise. In the end, the freehold went to a company in the north of England who also acted as managing agents – and the leaseholders have been complaining ever since.

GET MOVING!

If you ever get a chance like this, do your utmost to persuade the other residents to take it, as next time you want to enfranchise, prices will have gone up. It is common for developers to go bust and a very good time to buy the freehold.

It is also said that the longer the residents sit round a table and deliberate, the less the likelihood there is that they will ever get together to buy the freehold.

TIP

You will *definitely* need a specialist enfranchisement lawyer for this job. It is too complex, too user-unfriendly and too full of possible snags for it to be feasible for leaseholders to try to do it themselves. Since 2002, when the Commonhold and Leasehold Reform Act came in, many firms have been set up with the sole purpose of enabling leaseholders to enfranchise, and it may make sense to use one. It is important to try to get quotes, as some firms charge a flat fee, whereas others charge by the hour.

The CE process works like this:

1. After getting agreement from at least 50 per cent of long leaseholders in the building, setting up the company and getting the requisite valuations, you serve the enfranchisement notice on the freeholder.

2. The landlord then serves a counter notice.

3. If agreement cannot be reached, there is an application to the LVT. Note: the great majority of enfranchisements happen *without* recourse to the LVT. Why? Because it can involve the landlord in a lot of legal costs – costs he is usually most anxious to avoid.

4. The LVT hearing and decision takes place.

5. Completion of the freehold purchase.

The most cost-intensive and complicated of these steps is the first one, which is serving the notice. This notice is served by the Nominee Purchaser (the company set up by you, the leaseholders wishing to enfranchise) and includes the offer for the freehold, based on a professional valuation. This is in itself a specialised endeavour.

The notice must be signed by *all* the participants, and the landlord has two months to reply. In that time, the landlord has the right to inspect each participating flat and can demand access.

The second phase, where the landlord serves the counter notice, states whether the landlord accepts in principal that the leaseholders qualify to purchase and, if so, states his counter offer. If the landlord does not reply, the leaseholders can buy the freehold at the offer price.

If agreement cannot be reached, phase three – application to the LVT – comes into force. This means that the enfranchisers ask the LVT to set a reasonable price at which the landlord *must* sell.

The LVT is a quasi-judicial body, growing in size and importance all the time as ever more blocks of flats decide to enfranchise. At the hearing, it will give the price it deems 'reasonable' and this leads into phase five, which is completion of the freehold purchase.

At this stage, the landlord must prepare a contract and give it to the nominee purchaser within 21 days of the LVT hearing, or within 21 days of agreement with the purchaser.

Then the place is yours, forever.

TIPS ON DECIDING WHETHER OR NOT TO PROCEED WITH CE

Kat Callo offers these tips before deciding whether to proceed with CE:

> CE is not suitable for every block, so analyse whether this is the best option for your building. If so, circulate a business plan and time frame. Collect deposit payments from each participating resident. Project-manage stage by stage and be clear about latecomers. They had their chance – and now cannot be allowed to hold up proceedings.

Kat admits this can be difficult in the modern world, when some potential participants may be in Australia, climbing a mountain or otherwise uncontactable. Some residents may have died, and the flat now belongs to their estate. It is essential that all qualifying residents are contacted beforehand, and given a chance to participate. Therefore, you cannot proceed until everybody has been unearthed and contacted.

She adds:

Send regular update notes to all participants as CE proceeds. It is most important to keep all information confidential and away from the landlord. Talk is cheap – so don't talk about your CE to anybody except the participants. You have no need to keep the non-participants informed and you should not do so, as they may be spies for the landlord.

Just let the lawyers and experts handle it. Once a core group of you has decided to try and enfranchise, give people six weeks or so to respond, and then start the process.

What about the non-participants?

Once CE has been achieved, leases can be extended – for a nominal sum – to participants. This does not mean that non-participants, of whom there are always a few, will be allowed to extend their leases for nothing. What happens is that the Company set up by the Enfranchisers now owns the building, not the previous freeholder, and non-participants will retain their short leases. They have become, in effect, tenants of the company and they will not be allowed to own a share. This could make life difficult when they want to sell. Also, of course, they do not have a vote on management issues.

A more serious problem could be that when a building buys the freehold, this includes the non-participating flats, as the purchase price is for the whole block. In some cases, this may represent an insuperable financial stumbling block to purchase.

What usually happens is that the participants buy the freehold between them, and the non-participants are excluded. They are not part of the new company, or the new freehold.

Clearly, it is in everybody's interests to get as high a proportion of participants as possible. A common attitude, according to Alex Greenslade, of Leasehold Solutions, is for people to say, 'I'll do it if everybody else does.'

This is a common, if unhelpful, attitude, and often, reluctant participants need persuading of the advantages of enfranchising. This is where clear and regular communication comes in.

RUN THE COMPANY PROPERLY

Once you have enfranchised, it pays to appoint a professional company secretary, rather than try to do it yourself, as company law can be bewildering for the volunteer amateur. Remember, the company can be struck off and the properties revert to the Crown unless company law is obeyed to the letter, and the commonest companies to be struck off these days are recent enfranchisements. Company secretary work is often undertaken by firms of managing agents, at a cost of a few hundred pounds a year.

And unless there is only a very small number of individual flats in the block, it pays to appoint professional managing agents. The expert advice is: do not attempt to do it yourselves, even on a voluntary basis.

Do you now own the building between you?

Technically, no. The leaseholders own shares in the company which owns the block, and the company has an independent existence of its own.

The company formed to purchase the freehold is limited by guarantee, which means the members are guarantors of the company's debts, to a nominal sum. The directors of the company must carry out all the duties set out in the lease and raise money to pay for ongoing costs and future works.

Who are the directors?

As the new company is non-profit making, the directors will usually be volunteers who are in effect serving their neighbours. It can be difficult to persuade enough people to become directors, although, as Robert Levene of the Federation of Private Residents' Associations points out, this does not prevent non-directors from criticising those who do volunteer.

And finally...

Whether you are embarking on RTM or CE, it is most important to establish a sense of community before, during and afterwards. Otherwise, the situation could develop into a Mrs Merton-style 'heated debate' on every little issue. The best ways of establishing this feeling of togetherness is to have a regular newsletter or website whereby everybody is kept up to date. There must also be total transparency about costs, charges and company decisions.

This means that those appointed as directors or overseers must be people in whom the others have total trust.

6

Ex-local Authority Blocks

These are a law unto themselves and, accordingly, I have devoted a chapter to them.

The main difference between buying a flat in the private sector and ex-local authority stock is that in the former you are buying into a block which is predominately or entirely leasehold.

With local authority buildings by contrast, you are buying into a building with a mixture of leaseholders, private tenants and social tenants, and this intimately affects the way the building is run.

COLLECTIVE ENFRANCHISEMENT
It is widely believed that you cannot collectively enfranchise with an ex-local authority block. In fact, this is not entirely true, although it can be very difficult. But CE would be possible with, say, a block containing 18 flats, of which 14 are on a long leasehold. The bigger the block, the greater the problem.

But Richard Towes, Head of Home Ownership at the London Borough of Hammersmith and Fulham, says:

> We're more than happy to lose control of the building. In our borough, several blocks have already enfranchised, and the building has passed entirely into private ownership, meaning we have nothing more to do with it.

Where a block has enfranchised, but there remain council tenants, the council becomes a leaseholder, and pays service charges to the new freeholder. In other words, the role is reversed, and the council would have to buy the new lease from the enfranchisers instead of the other way round.

LEASES SHORTER THAN 80 YEARS

This is a common problem within this sector. When a former council tenant buys a lease from the council, this is for 125 years.

In normal cases, this can be extended for 90 years as it starts to run down – in the same way as in the private sector – for a suitable fee. This means that most leaseholders in these blocks have nothing to worry about.

But when it comes to high-rise blocks built in the 1960s, and the council may be the head leaseholder, rather than the outright owner, problems can occur. For one thing, the original leases granted to the council may have been shorter than 125 years, so by the time the council tenant comes to exercise right to buy, they could have become very short indeed.

Example

There are three high-rise blocks opposite Shepherd's Bush station, in West London. These were originally built by a private company which wanted to develop commercial property in the area. The council on this occasion insisted that at the same time they built residential accommodation for social tenants. The property developer remained the freeholder.

In time, a proportion of these social tenants exercised their right to buy. But because the council was the head leaseholder, rather than the freeholder, they had less control over length or extension of the leases. This has resulted in some leases becoming very short indeed, under 70 years. In addition, it is difficult, if not impossible, to get a mortgage for higher than the seventh floor in blocks of this type.

Again, Richard Towes explains:

> Where we are not the freeholders, as in these blocks, we cannot grant a longer lease. But as the law allows a leaseholder to extend the lease, we have to refer potential buyers to the freeholder. Potential buyers have to be very aware of the sell-on possibilities in blocks of this type.

All over the country, there are high-rise ex-council blocks where the council is not the owner. This is something to find out before buying, as very often these blocks are in wonderful locations and have stupendous views.

Also, contrary to popular belief, many are extremely well kept, with concierge services 24 hours a day, 365 days a year.

A NOTE ON MORTGAGES

Council tenants living in high-rise blocks who want to exercise their right to buy at a discount normally have no difficulty in obtaining an ex-local authority mortgage.

Problems arise when that leaseholder comes to sell and the property goes onto the open market. Many property investors buy these flats to rent out, knowing that they have a wasting asset, but calculating that the rent payable for the life of the lease still gives them a considerable profit on the investment.

Increasingly, local authorities supply an information pack for new owners which sets out all the terms under which they have bought the lease.

SOCIAL TENANTS

Most local authority blocks will contain a proportion of social tenants. These are people who, for one reason or another, do not have the means to go into the private sector. This is what social housing is all about, and anybody buying into a local authority block must be aware of this. Some of these blocks may never pass into predominately private ownership. On a small estate where I have an ex-council flat, there are just 12 leaseholders among 80 flats, and this percentage has not changed for years.

SERVICE CHARGES

These are levied according to a different principle from the private sector in that local authorities are not allowed to amass a sinking fund. This means that service charges can seem extremely cheap.

When you buy from a local authority, the information pack should state this, saying that you the leaseholder will be liable for your share of any major works.

Richard Towes says: 'Local authorities are not allowed to hold money in trust, as in the private sector. This means that whenever there are major works, leaseholders can suddenly be clobbered for large bills.'

The reason for this is the presence of the council tenants. If you have 10 leaseholders and 40 council tenants in a block of 50 flats, the local authority is not in a position to put money into the sinking fund on behalf of the rent payers.

Richard Towes continues:

> When former council tenants buy a lease, they have to start paying service charges, which did not happen before. We point out that their share could be a lot of money. Nowadays, this is made abundantly clear, although it was not always spelt out in the past, which is why there have been so many stories of ex-council leaseholders suddenly having to find four- and five-figure sums.

It has to be said that local authorities are now getting much better at keeping leaseholders informed about service charges and how they are apportioned. In most cases, leaseholders receive a booklet each year with their service charge bill, setting out each element of the cost.

Another way in which service charges in this sector differ is that they are levied in arrears, not in advance. You pay for services already supplied. It is the same with major works. The council borrows money to carry out major works, such as installing new windows in the whole block, and you are billed maybe two or three years later.

But all leaseholders have to be circulated with the estimates and quotations in advance, with an accurate estimate of their share of the cost.

For instance, I was billed just over £2,000 for my share of new windows in my ex-local authority block, years after their installation. But I was informed of the quotations in advance.

There was nothing I could do about it, although as a leaseholder I do have the legal right to take any charge I feel to be 'unreasonable' to the LVT. Not all local authority leaseholders realise they have this right, but the law does try to be even-handed on this matter.

A bone of contention is that whereas leaseholders pay service charges and for major works, council tenants pay nothing on top of their subsidised rent. But councils argue that council tenants do pay, and that their rent goes towards all these costs.

Summary

To sum up: the main difference regarding service charges is that in the private sector, leaseholders put money in before the works are carried out, whereas with council blocks, the local authority does the works, then bills the leaseholder.

For those who cannot pay a single large sum, most councils have schemes in place whereby leaseholders can pay over five years – with interest added, of course. Or they can pay over one year, without interest added.

Any leaseholder having difficulty with paying a one-off sum for major works should contact the relevant authority and work out a payment plan together.

There is also the fact that in the private sector, the aim is to make a profit, but local authorities are not allowed to make a profit. So when major works are indicated, the council do not take an extra ten per cent commission.

Richard Towes says:

> The private sector landlord often has another building and maintenance company, and gets a kickback from this. We are not allowed to do this. It is also not always realised that leaseholders are entitled to nominate their own contractor if they do not like our estimate for works.

RESIDENTS' ASSOCIATIONS

Many local authority blocks and estates have thriving Residents' Associations. These have to register with the local authority and be open to all residents, tenants or leaseholders to join.

The Association must also have a proper constitution. Nowadays, many local boroughs have Federations of Residents' Associations and run regular forums for these Associations in their area.

There is also likely to be a leaseholders' panel which all leaseholders are invited to join. These Associations are important as many issues that arise concern tenants and leaseholders alike, such as security, gardening, state of common areas or caretaking.

BREACH OF LEASE

Local authorities can take exactly the same action for breaches of lease as the private sector. Where there is a dispute, a leaseholder can be taken to court, to the LVT or expect a visit from a debt collection agency.

INVESTMENT VALUE

It is still the case that an ex-local authority flat will tend to be cheaper than an identical flat in an equivalent area which is not local authority. There is a slight remaining stigma regarding these flats, although it is lessening all the time.

But the presence of the social tenants means that the value is always likely to be lower.

IS THERE A BEST BUY?

The best bargains, in my view, are to be found in so-called 'gap sites', where the council has built a small block of less than 20 properties in the gap between other housing. Although these buildings are not as pretty as the surrounding houses – for example, you often see a 'gap site' in a row of pretty Victorian cottages – they are often in brilliant locations and once you are inside, you can forget about it being ex-council.

Ex-council flats are often very well designed and spacious. But they do need a lot of help to obtain a designer feel and make them chic.

The most difficult buys are those on huge estates, where the difference in price is astonishing, compared to a non-council property in the same area. For instance, a large four-bedroom ex-council flat on the White City estate, near to the BBC, costs (at the time of writing) £220,000, whereas the same size property in the private sector only two streets away costs at least £500,000. Yes, you get a bargain – but will it increase significantly in value and how long will you have to wait for this to happen? In the meantime, you are living in the middle of a vast council estate, which is not everybody's idea of an ideal location.

Property investors are snapping up ex-council flats fast, believing that if the location is good, they will one day be extremely valuable. But you need a strong head and a long time frame. From a buy-to-let perspective, snapping up one of these large flats can make a lot of sense, as you get exactly the same rent for a bargain four-bedroom council flat as for an expensive four-bedroom Victorian terrace house in the next street.

Letting a Flat

Buy-to-let has become so popular that many people imagine it's easy enough to buy a flat and rent it out.

In fact, the vast majority of residential leases impose restrictions on renting out, or subletting as it is known, and you would be wise to consult the lease before ever making an offer on a buy-to-let apartment.

THE LEASE

Whenever considering buying a flat to rent out to others, make sure you look carefully at the lease first, as there may well be restrictions.

Some leases insist of rentals on no less than a year, very many leases forbid short lets and whatever the lease may say, it is against the law in the UK to rent out a flat as a home for less than 90 days at a stretch. Holiday lets are another matter, as they are considered leisure activities and not homes.

Even where you have bought a flat with a share of the freehold, these same restrictions will apply. And with newbuilds, where most buy-to-let investments are made, the property is rarely sold with a share of the freehold.

Even if the flat is commonhold, similar strictures will apply on subletting. It is important to bear in mind that you the landlord, or leaseholder, are ultimately responsible for what goes on inside your property not your tenant.

When it comes to renting out an apartment abroad, the situation can get even more complicated, as some apartment buildings do not allow any form of subletting, whereas in other apartment buildings you are not allowed to rent out to holidaymakers, in case it takes away from local trade.

RESTRICTIVE SUBLETTING

What does it all mean in practice, especially as around 30 per cent of all new flats in the UK are now being bought specifically by investors with renting out in mind?

And why do so many leases impose subletting restrictions?

A major issue here is that of security, which is always of the utmost importance in any apartment building. The more unknown people there are going in and out, the greater the security risk.

Another factor is that of keeping a check on the behaviour of occupants, as when there are many subtenants in a place, it becomes difficult to track perpetrators of the kind of bad behaviour which is so intolerable in a block of flats, such as loud music, rubbish left in corridors, washing hanging out of windows and front doors being left wide open.

There is also the question of value, as some freeholders believe that an apartment building loses value when it contains more sub-tenants than owner-occupiers and becomes in effect a rooming-house. The greatest fear is that transient tenants will not look after the place, as they have no great interest in the common parts or the fabric of the building.

Relevant clauses

So, first check the relevant clauses to establish the following:

- Is any kind of subletting actually allowed on the lease? Some leases do not allow subletting *at all*.
- If subletting is permitted, are there any restrictions on length of tenure and type of tenant?
- Do you have to give details of the tenant to the freeholder or managing agent?
- Are holiday lets allowed?
- Are short lets allowed?
- Are you expected to be responsible for your tenants' behaviour?
- Are pets allowed?
- Is smoking allowed?

Also bear in mind that in residential accommodation, tenants are not allowed to carry on a business from their home. Obviously this is in many ways a grey area but the usual interpretation is that you are allowed to be a writer or illustrator, say, from home, but you are not allowed to run a business where people may be coming to your home. Therefore tenants would not be allowed to offer a holistic massage service or run a reflexology or acupuncture clinic from their home.

In general, 'running a business' means you are not allowed to carry on any commercial activity which involves either clients coming to your home, or where business equipment would have to be installed.

The effect of ignoring restrictive subletting

Remember that any persistent flouting of these clauses will result in a breach of the lease and could, in extreme cases, lead to forfeiture, meaning that you, the investor, end up with nothing, regardless of how long the lease is and however much you paid for it. After all, if the matter comes to court, it will be argued that you agreed to the terms of a legally-binding agreement when you signed the lease.

The lease is paramount when you are renting properties out, in just the same way as when you are living there yourself.

WHAT KIND OF SUBLETTING IS ALLOWED?

The Assured Shorthold Tenancy

In most apartment blocks, only Assured Shorthold Tenancies (AST), of six months or more, are allowed. Many blocks will only allow subtenancies of one year or more.

The AST is the commonest type of tenancy in existence today and means that the property is rented out for one year minimum, with a break clause after six months.

Terms of the tenancy are set out in the tenancy agreement, which both you and the tenant must sign. These are standard agreements, obtainable from most stationers and also drawn up by professional letting agents if you take that route of finding a tenant. It is usually best to use a letting agent that is a member of the Association of Residential Letting Agents (ARLA), which has much useful advice you can download from their website (www.arla.com).

Holiday lets, defined as lettings of one month or less, are not usually allowed anyway as most residential leases state that no commercial business is to be carried on within the building. Holiday lets, as opposed to ASTs, count as running a business. Other types of letting are considered unearned income, as with investments and savings, and taxed accordingly.

In some cases, regardless of what the lease may permit, the local borough will not allow lets of less than a certain length of time, in case this takes away from the hotel trade. In the London boroughs of Westminster and Kensington and Chelsea, for instance, lets of less than three months are not permitted.

CASE STUDY

Campden Hill Towers, a large 1960s block in Notting Hill, West London, had become home to a large amount of extremely transient tenants, many only staying for a weekend. Eventually the Residents' Association mounted a tough campaign, with the result that only lettings of 12 months or more were to be permitted.

In addition, all tenant references had to be lodged with the managing agents, and a photograph of each occupant given to the resident porter. A photo of each subtenant had also to be given to the managing agents.

Sub-subletting

Remember always that whatever else may be allowed or otherwise on the lease, in law a subtenant is *never* allowed to sub-sublet, or to allow people to live in the flat who are not specifically named on the tenancy agreement.

Nowadays, most managing agents or freeholders insist on having the names of tenants, contact numbers and a key to the property so they can be contacted at any time. It is very common for absentee landlords to be out of the country most of the time, and not to take much interest in the day-to-day affairs of the tenants in their investment property.

Such negligence has got absentee landlords a bad name which is quite often justified.

BUYING A FLAT TO LET

Ever more people are buying flats simply in order to let them, with no intention of ever living in the place themselves. It is not unusual these days to hear of quite ordinary people owning literally hundreds of properties which they sublet to tenants paying rent.

But even when you are an absentee landlord, you remain responsible for the property, for paying the service charges, ground rent and any building levies or other costs imposed by the freeholder or managing agents.

If there is bad behaviour by your tenants, the freeholder or Residents' Association will come on to *you*, not your tenant, to sort it out.

Financing the purchase

Unless paying cash, you will have to set up a special buy-to-let mortgage as, strictly speaking, you are not allowed to sublet on an ordinary mortgage. Most investors take out interest-only mortgages and hope that the rental income will more than cover costs such as mortgage repayments, letting fees and any other costs.

There are currently more than 50 lenders offering buy-to-let mortgages and the business is becoming very competitive indeed, so it pays to shop around. There will also be setting-up fees and survey fees to pay.

In general, the mortgage is granted on the amount of rent the property is expected to fetch, rather than your income levels. The usual ratio is that the rent must cover 130 per cent of the mortgage repayment costs. Usually you would have to put down a 20 per cent deposit in cash.

It is vital, before buying an investment flat, to work out all the figures, and see whether they give you an operating profit, bearing in mind – as we have already seen – that buying into an apartment building can have ongoing costs so far as service charges, ground rent, building levies and other maintenance costs are concerned. There will also be insurance, fees to letting agents, cost of upgrading or updating, phone calls to tenants, petrol, as well as the possibility of unpaid rent.

So, make sure you know precisely what you are getting into, and work out the figures as exactly as you can. Wishful thinking is to be discouraged, especially as tenants now have many properties to choose from, and there is great competition in the marketplace. Very few of today's highly-geared landlords can afford a void, whereby the property will not rent out at all. And if you have to keep reducing the rent, you may find you can no longer cover costs.

Proceed on all the certainties you can – rather than just hoping it will all work out.

Your responsibilities as a landlord

Many amateur investors buy flats and rent them out without ever considering that by doing so they are involving themselves in highly complicated tenure matters.

Very many property clubs and expensive buy-to-let seminars never ever mention this aspect of buy-to-let, as they concentrate only on the possible profit to be made from tenants. But when you house somebody, you have assumed a certain amount of responsibility for that person.

Buying a flat to let is emphatically not the same as setting up a car hire business, for instance, as when you provide a roof over somebody's head, that somebody has rights as well as you – rights that in some cases go back to ancient times.

All the rules and regulations affecting both sides to the contract – that is, the landlord and the tenant – will be set out in the legally-binding tenancy agreement. Make sure you understand and agree to all the terms before signing such a document.

You will, for instance, need to ensure that all furnishings and fittings meet current health and safety requirements and that gas and electrical fittings and appliances also conform to present day standards. It is mandatory to have an annual gas check, and also to have any new electrical installations fitted by an Approved Contractor who will issue the relevant certificate.

In addition, you will have to compile an inventory – this is not as difficult as some people make it seem but essential none the less – and deal with matters such as the dilapidations deposit and receiving the rent on time.

You may also need extra insurance when renting out a property in an apartment block.

CARRYING OUT BUILDING WORK

Planning permission
If your flat needs a lot of renovation before being ready to rent out, you must obtain the relevant permissions before work starts. Here, you should obtain quotes, then send these to the freeholder, managing agents or Residents' Association, giving details of the work and length of time they are likely to take.

You must also contact the local council to see whether any planning permission or building consents are required, or whether building regulations apply to the kind of work you are considering. A reputable firm of builders should be able to do this for you, but first of all you would need to know from the freeholder that you are allowed to carry out these works in principle. If so, write a standard letter to the freeholder, managing agents and other occupants giving details of the works, name and contact details of the contractors, and length of time the work is likely to take.

If the building is listed, you will have to obtain listed building consent in addition to all the other consents.

If other residents believe you have not obtained the relevant permissions and consents, they could well cause work to be stopped.

There are now extremely strict rules regarding soundproofing in blocks of flats, given that the most common complaint is of noise nuisance coming from flats above and below. The fact that you will not be there yourself to hear the noise or even live in the place is beside the point.

Being responsible

You should also reassure residents that the site will be left clean and tidy each evening and that works will not be carried out at night or on Sundays. Check with your freeholder or managing agents as to whether planning permission is required, as there may be strict rules about alteration, knocking two flats into one, or turning one flat into two, for instance.

CASE STUDY

Tina, an amateur property investor, bought two studio flats next to each other in a Knightsbridge mansion block, with the intention of turning them into one bigger flat. Some residents saw what was going on and reported her to the managing agents, who took her to court. At the hearing, she was ordered to turn her property back into two flats, as this type of alteration was not allowed in the lease. It had simply not occurred to Tina either to check her lease or ask permission for the alterations and the experience cost her very dear indeed.

Unless you obtain proper consents, the return on your investment could suffer very badly indeed. Whatever happens, do not buy a derelict or unmodernised flat and barge in, knocking walls down and piling up sacks of rubble outside in corridors before getting all the relevant permissions and consents.

BEING A GOOD (ABSENTEE) LANDLORD

The most hated owners of all in apartment blocks are the absentee landlords who, next to the subtenants, tend to be blamed for everything bad that happens to the building. Many owner-occupiers believe that their building will soon become derelict if infested by enough absentee landlords and investors who couldn't care less. Don't confirm their prejudices.

Make sure that the managing agents of the block have your address and details and how you can be contacted in an emergency. And do, if possible, attend AGMS and EGMs as this will enable owner-occupiers to put a name to the face and it will also show them that you care.

If possible, agree to become a voluntary director, or a committee member. Nothing endears you more to the other owners. They are so grateful that somebody other than themselves will agree to take responsibility for the smooth running of the block that they will forgive you for being one of those nasty get-rich-quick investors.

FINDING TENANTS

There are many categories of tenant, and you will have to decide which type best suits your property or location. Tenants can be singles, couples, sharers or families and each property will attract a particular type of tenant. In general, flats are not usually suitable for families and, indeed, leases in some very upmarket blocks may not permit children, let alone pets.

Letting agents will advise on which areas and types of property attract particular tenants. The student market is growing all the time, and there are now purpose-built blocks aimed entirely at student occupation, where you can buy a flat – or maybe several – as an investor.

The student market, though, is very different from other markets and the best advice here would be to contact your local university lodgings department and ask for a copy of their landlords' booklet. You are not usually allowed to set your own rents, for instance, but have to abide by the amounts set down in the booklet.

Using a letting agency

If you are buying on a mortgage, you will be required to use a reputable letting agent who will advertise the property, find and vet tenants, take the dilapidations deposit under the Tenancy Deposit Scheme, carry out reference checks, draw up the tenancy agreement, set up the standing order and check that the flat complies with the current health and safety regulations.

Going it alone

If you own the property outright you can, if you like, advertise it yourself. Around 50 per cent of landlords decide to go it alone and save themselves the expense of a letting agent. As always, there are pros and cons. However many layers you like to put between yourself and your tenant, you have to remember that the contract is between you and the tenant, and not between the tenant and the agency.

If you are finding tenants privately, you will have to show them round the flat and check and vet them yourself. Yes you can save yourself the ten per cent (plus VAT) commission, but it is a lot of hard work, especially if you have a full-time job as well.

Full management or not?

Letting agents can handle every aspect of finding tenants such as drawing up tenancy agreements, taking the deposit, setting up the standing order, compiling the inventory, checking tenants in and checking out. They can also arrange for repairs, for eviction of bad tenants, collection of rent and redecoration.

But all these services come at extra cost. Most agents have a scale of fees ranging from ten per cent for finding and checking out a tenant, to 15–20 per cent for full management or even more for organising holiday lets.

I would say that for ordinary tenancies you do not need to go for the full management option as in the scheme of things, the vast majority of tenancies are trouble free. With the ten per cent service, the agent withdraws once the tenancy arrangements have been completed and plays no further part in the operation.

For all levels of service, the letting agent will do a reference and credit check, make sure there is enough income to pay the rent, take and hold the deposit and show prospective tenants round. They will insist that all health and safety measures are kept and that all furniture and fittings comply with current regulations. Otherwise they will refuse to act for you as by so doing they may be breaking the law.

Full management means that the property will be checked once a month, and any repairs carried out immediately – in theory at least. For this, the agency will ask for a float to cover these costs. Typically you will be charged the cost of the repair or other work, plus ten per cent agency fee on top. VAT comes on top of all quoted prices.

Full management is probably necessary if you are abroad or unobtainable, but bear in mind that even the fullest management service does not operate at night or at weekends.

YOUR TENANT'S RESPONSIBILITIES
The tenant is responsible for paying the rent, all utilities, the council tax and also telephone and other connection charges plus the television licence. You the owner remain responsible for the service charges.

Keeping your tenant informed

It is a very good idea to give your tenant a simplified form of the lease, as there can then be no excuse for infringing any of its clauses. Some firms of managing agents now provide these simplified leases, especially for tenants.

In flats, it is also essential to provide a fire extinguisher and blanket, and supply your tenant with information on the fire drill.

The tenant should have details of the managing agents, caretaker, cleaners and anybody else responsible for running the block.

TIP

Some freeholders charge you the leaseholder a small sum to register each tenant. Local councils are fond of doing this. You must inform the freeholder or managing agents of all changes of tenancy.

TYPES OF TENANCY

The AST (Assured Shorthold Tenancy), is governed by the Housing Act of 1989 and has proved very successful ever since. On an AST you can have corporate tenants, sharers, young professionals, students, couples, families or singles. The only proviso for setting up an AST is that the flat must be self-contained and have its own front door.

Many agents will not consider flats in attics or basements, for instance, where you would have to go through the main flat to get to the secondary flat.

SHORT LETS

Are they allowed?
Short lets, of less than six months, can be very profitable, as the rents are much higher. *But*, before ever embarking on a short let, check that these are allowed by both the freeholder and the local council. Some boroughs stipulate that all lets must be at least six months in length.

If allowed, they are useful when:

◆ you are going away yourself on an extended holiday or short job contract and need to somehow pay the mortgage in the meantime;

◆ you cannot let out your flat on the usual AST;

◆ you have the property up for sale and want to sell with vacant possession.

Your responsibilities as a short let landlord
Short lets come into a special category of their own, and not all agents handle them. Agents specialising in short let provide short let information packs, which you should obtain and read carefully beforehand.

With short lets, you the landlord are expected to provide everything in the property; including towels, linen, cutlery and all furniture and fittings. As with ASTs, all furniture should be compliant and all fittings must meet current safety requirements.

The short let agency will take the entire rent plus deposit upfront and also deduct tax at source before passing any money on to you.

This is a legal requirement.

You as the landlord will also retain responsibility for utility bills, and reputable agencies make stringent checks to ensure the short-let tenant does not suddenly double the use of gas and electricity. There will also be strict rules governing telephone, internet and cable or satellite use.

You are also required to inform your mortgage lender of any subletting, including a short let.

Short lets operate at all levels of the market and even quite ordinary flats can be popular. But remember that even if the lease permits these lets, some local boroughs do not allow them as they are seen to be taking away hotel trade.

HOLIDAY LETS

Are they allowed?
Most residential leases emphatically do not allow holiday lets, defined as lets of one month or less. This is because they are considered a business and, as such, come under different tax rules than ASTs or short lets, where the profit is considered to be unearned income. Holiday lets, again, are not allowed on many leases for the same reason as short lets, plus the fact that in some buildings you are not allowed to be carrying on a business.

Holiday lets are not covered by the various Housing Acts as these lets are supposed to be for a genuine holiday rather than providing somebody with a home.

If allowed, make no mistake, holiday lets are hard work! Most visitors will stay for no longer than two weeks, and if the let is for more than four weeks it cannot count as a holiday let. You have to provide everything down to the last teaspoon, and have the place thoroughly and professionally cleaned after each let. These days, it is not unknown for holidaymakers to book a flat just for a weekend which increases wear and tear on the property.

Although holiday lets command maybe three times the rental of ASTs, they are easily six times the work. Also, it is unlikely the flat will be let year-round. With holiday lets, you have to take all the rental money upfront, plus a large deposit which is returned at the end of the holiday.

Do not ever try holiday lets without confirming that this is allowed under the lease. Most Residents' Associations frown on holiday lets and short lets and, under extreme circumstances, persistent offenders could have their leases forfeited.

The main reason for this is the issue of security and of not knowing who is coming in and out of the building, and who has a key.

CASE STUDY

One investor in my building applied for permission to rent out his flat as a holiday let rather than on an AST. Because he had previously proved himself an excellent landlord, we the directors gave him personal written permission to do this, with the proviso that the concession could be withdrawn at any time. We also made it clear that this concession did not go with the property, but was personal to him only.

When he put the flat on the market, he applied for permission for the property to continue to be used for holiday lets. But because we did not know anything about the new buyer, this permission was withheld. In the end, he sold it to an owner-occupier and we all breathed a hearty sigh of relief.

LEASING TO A HOUSING ASSOCIATION OR LOCAL COUNCIL

Many letting agents do not handle this sector, but social tenants exist and are getting more numerous. Also, to be realistic, in some areas this is the only tenant pool there is.

Here again, you must first obtain permission from the freeholder or Residents' Association as in this case you would be leasing your flat to the social landlord for maybe three to five years, and they will be housing people who are 'in need' rather than those who might be wonderful tenants.

Accordingly, the checks that are made before ordinary tenants move in, are not made, as the only criterion is that of 'need'. And once you have leased your property to the social landlord, you absolve all responsibility for it for the duration of the agreement.

But beware because again, you could be served with a forfeiture notice if your social tenants are persistently badly behaved.

Many landlords like leasing to social landlords because they get a good deal, which may include a golden hello and cleaning and decorating of the property. There is no commission to pay, there are no agents' fees, and the rent is guaranteed – whether or not the social landlord or tenant receives it.

LETTING OUT YOUR OWN HOME

Strictly speaking, you are not allowed to rent out your own home on a homebuyer's mortgage, but must have a proper buy-to-let mortgage in place. However, if you are going on an extended holiday or work project for three months or so, it is not feasible to keep chopping and changing mortgage types.

However, you should always let your mortgage provider know, as you may not be insured if anything happens while you are not living there yourself.

Also, all the usual rules apply when renting out your own home such as, does the lease allow short lets or holiday lets?

If letting your own home through an agency, you will have to ensure that all furniture, fittings, appliances and certificates are in place, just as you would with specific buy-to-let.

It is very common these days for flat owners – especially young flat owners – to want to rent out their flats while on work assignments abroad. This enables them to keep their home and pay the mortgage.

But you would have to ensure that the property meets current regulations and requirements.

Never let to friends

And please, please do not ever be tempted to do things cheaply and let in an ad-hoc fashion to friends. Although this advice also applies when renting out a freehold house, it becomes ever more urgent when it comes to leasehold flats. You may be reluctant to set up a formal type of tenancy with a friend and not bother with an inventory, or you may consider it a breach of friendship and trust to give them a version of the lease. And if they then breach any terms, you may find it difficult to tell them about it.

If you are tempted to let out your flat to a friend, make sure you treat them exactly as you would a stranger, otherwise, don't take the risk.

TAX MATTERS

If you earn any rental income at all from your flat, you will have to declare this to the Inland Revenue and pay tax accordingly. When renting out a flat on an AST or short let, you can claim letting fees, inventory fees, ten per cent wear and tear, repairs and refurbishment and also service charges and ground rent.

You may in addition be able to claim travel and telephone costs, plus the costs of recovering unpaid rent.

As holiday lets are counted as a business, they are taxed as such, therefore you can claim many more things, but the flat has to be available to let for 140 days a year and actually let for 70 of those days to count as a genuine business.

When you sell a flat that is not your main home you will be liable for Capital Gains Tax of up to 40 per cent on the profit made. This is the capital profit, not on income from rentals. But there are many things you can set against this tax such as cost of renovation, building levies and installing central heating or new windows, for instance.

It is always a good idea to take professional advice about tax matters, as you also incur tax liability if you are letting property abroad or if you live in another country but remain a UK citizen.

$$\binom{8}{}$$

When Things Go Wrong

Whenever you drive or walk past a block of flats, it all looks calm and serene. How nice, you might imagine, to have a flat in this lovely block by the river, or in that gorgeous trendy building with its underground carpark and residents' swimming pool.

Yet the chances are that if you were to buy a flat in one of those appealing-looking blocks, you would very likely discover you had bought into an ongoing soap opera or dark sitcom, with deadly feuds, splinter groups, and endless lawsuits raging therein.

Problems are endemic to blocks of flats, for two reasons: the first is that because everybody is interdependent, anything going wrong in one flat, such as a leaking tap or pipe, is eventually likely to affect many other flats. The second reason is that blocks of flats contain many disparate people who may have nothing whatsoever in common with each other and, as a result, there may be many personality clashes. Blocks of flats contain people who may not normally choose to live together, actually having to live on top of one another.

And not all the rules and regulations in the world will prevent leaking pipes and personality clashes. Although leases draw up a kind of two-way contract between the leaseholder and the freeholder, with the aim of benefitting both, there is no documentation which determines how the inhabitants should treat each other.

Problems in blocks of flats are mainly caused by:

◆ Non-payers.
◆ Absentee leaseholders not caring.
◆ Lots of subtenants in a block.
◆ Lack of professional managing agents.
◆ Freeholders who can't be bothered.
◆ Lack of money for essential maintenance.
◆ Large numbers of elderly residents who can't afford or don't want to enfranchise or pay for repairs.
◆ Leaseholders falling out among themselves.

THESE ARE THE BEST SOLUTIONS

1. Appoint professional managing agents

Disputes between residents in blocks of flats have escalated mightily since it became possible to collectively enfranchise and secure the RTM. Once they have secured either or both of these rights, residents often imagine it will save money and make life easier if they managed the place themselves. This is almost always a mistake and a false economy. Residents are much less likely to make a fuss and refuse to pay if they receive official-looking demands from a professional company, and can contact the managing agents direct.

The other problem is that self-managers are usually voluntary and, as such, are only prepared to give a certain amount of time to administration. In addition, there may not be anybody in the block who is fully conversant with the ramifications and complexities of leasehold law, who can keep tabs on accounts, and also appease any complainers.

The Citizens Advice Bureau – who are often the first port of call for aggrieved residents – confirms that disputes between leaseholders have increased mightily since more blocks enfranchised.

2. Communicate!

Residents need explanations and to be kept informed of what is going on. Directors and committee members have not signed the official secrets act, and must make all their doings and deliberations public. It is a good idea either to have a regular newsletter or a website whereby residents can be kept informed of work in progress, make suggestions or air their grievances.

A regular newsletter will establish a sense of community and make everybody feel they have a voice. A website is also an excellent idea, provided that somebody takes responsibility for keeping it up to date – there is nothing more annoying than an out-of-date website. Also make sure your newsletter or website is interactive and does not give the impression of commandments being handed down on tablets of stone from on high.

It is also a good idea to have a big noticeboard in the hall whereby residents can be kept informed. Residents can also pin items of interest up on the board, such as notices of local concerts, talks, services or cuttings from newspapers. This all gives a sense of community to the building.

Be careful, though, that the noticeboard does not just become a place for free advertisements and cards from contractors, IT consultants and builders.

3. Attend to small jobs instantly

All buildings often develop small problems which, if unattended, can easily turn into major tasks. Whenever you notice a small problem, such as rubbish or builder's rubble being left out in corridors, or washing hanging out, point it out to the managing agents or caretaker or attend to it yourself, before it gets any worse.

4. Put up pictures in the common parts

If you have leftover pictures, put them up in the halls and corridors. This immediately makes the place seem much more friendly, and less daunting and forbidding. The best kind of picture for this are local landscapes and scenes (prints rather than the real thing) that are intended to be glimpsed at in passing, rather than studied intently. Acres of bare wall are offputting and can give a prison-like atmosphere to a large block.

5. Hold regular meetings

Residents are all paying out what they consider to be large sums of money, and often feel that their money is being spent – or squandered – around them and without due consultation. It is good practice to hold an EGM whenever there are large jobs in the offing.

But *do not*, as sometimes happens, get into cliques or huddles, and invite some residents, but not others, to 'informal meetings'. It creates a bad atmosphere and encourages splinter groups which are the last thing you want. Everything should be democratic. Where there is a Board of voluntary Directors, as there will be after enfranchisement, these directors should also meet regularly.

All meetings should be property minuted. The idea is that everything and everybody should be accountable.

Wherever possible, hold meetings in a neutral venue, such as a church or school hall, or nearby hotel if funds will run to it.

Those who do not attend meetings cannot expect to have a voice. If you want your views to be heard, attend the meeting. AGMs and EGMs are notorious for poor attendance; then people moan and complain when their views are not recognised.

6. Hold social events regularly

Parties and events, such as a firework party, carol singing or a summer barbecue can all help to establish a sense of community and friendship. One large block of flats has established a library in the hall, whereby residents exchange books. It is just a simple idea but immediately gives the place a kind of village atmosphere.

It is also a good idea to 'deck the hall' at Christmas – put up a Christmas tree and decorations to give a festive feel. But make sure they are always taken down by Twelfth Night at the latest.

I have seen blocks of flats where brown Christmas trees – still with bits of tinsel clinging to them – have lain around in basements until August.

7. Lift a finger to help

Many residents keep complaining that 'they' – ie, the managing agents or Residents' Committee – do nothing. But ask yourself: what can I do? Some people may be interested in gardening, hanging pictures in common parts, doing some interior painting, or polishing up the brass. Instead of waiting for 'them' to do the small jobs, do them yourself! Although managing agents will oversee the management of the building, there will always be small day-to-day jobs that need doing, as with any property.

So, why wait for somebody else to do the work?

8. Do not contravene the terms of the lease

Before buying any flat, look carefully at the terms of the lease and once you've moved in, make sure you abide by them. For instance, do not hang washing over the balcony if this is expressly forbidden, do not lay laminate flooring where it says carpet, or leave windows dirty for years on end.

If you want the block of flats to be run efficiently, ensure you do your part by obeying the terms of the lease – never mind what others might do. Human beings are notorious copiers, and copy others' behaviour, whether this is good or bad.

When I first moved to my block, there were no pictures at all in the common parts. I decided to hang some that were surplus to my requirements, and they immediately pulled the place together and made it look at if somebody cared. Now, the common parts are a veritable art gallery – and the presence of the pictures somehow prevents people from leaving bags of rubbish out in the corridors as before.

The motto is: whatever you want doing, set a precedent by doing it yourself.

Somebody else put potted plants outside on the porch. Before long, others had followed suit, so that now we have a welcoming flower display by the entrances. This also has the happy result that people no longer dump rubbish in the porches.

9. Keep some money by

As with any property, there will always be unexpected costs when buying a flat. It is madness to stretch yourself so far when buying that you have nothing left over for repairs, your share of major or minor works to the building or an unexpected hike in service charges.

Almost all the long-term problems that arise in blocks of flats occur because some of the residents cannot pay their share, as they are already mortgaged or indebted up to the hilt. If you really will have nothing left after buying, look for something cheaper, or wait until you have managed to save up for, if not exactly a rainy day, at least the occasional shower. When a building falls into disrepair or loses value, this is almost always because a number of residents have been unable or unwilling to pay their share, and for this reason, essential works have never been carried out. This, as much as leases running down, makes the flats lose value.

Before ever buying a flat, work out all the figures, such as council tax, mortgage repayments and service charges. Then add something on for unexpected costs so that there will always be a reserve fund.

And whereas with a freehold house you have a choice as to whether to carry out works, with a flat you have no such choice because of the intimate interconnection between all the occupants. As a houseowner, you might choose to let your roof fall in; you cannot allow the roof to fall in on other people.

10. If you are an absentee landlord, play your part

Many buy-to-let landlords, wanting to maximise their profits, are unwilling to put their hands in their pockets to pay for repairs and renovations. Be careful that you are not seen to be using the building as a cash cow, or relying on the other residents' contributions to further your property development. This will not only make you wildly unpopular but could mean your investment goes down in value. Badly-managed blocks soon get a negative reputation with local estate agents, who may be unwilling to take a flat in such a block onto their books.

Also make sure that the managing agents have details of all your tenants; their names, contact numbers and details.

Plus, give your tenant a simplified form of the lease. Subtenants are almost always blamed for problems in blocks of flats; make sure your tenants are not among them.

11. Make sure somebody, either the caretaker or a neighbour, has a spare key

There are always times when it might be necessary to get into your flat; to investigate a leak, check wiring, cables or pipework. Problems can develop when you are on holiday or otherwise away, so ensure that access can be gained at all times.

12. Establish a policy of zero tolerance

If you have a policy that bikes and pushchairs are not to be left in the hall, put up a notice warning occupants that these objects will, if found, be taken outside. Then carry out the threat. Otherwise, there will soon be ten bikes left in the hall.

But, whenever punitive action is to be taken for misdemeanours, you should first give not only warnings, but reasons for the ban. For instance, you should say that bikes and pushchairs left in the hall constitute a fire hazard and invalidate the block insurance policy. Then you have a valid reason for taking direct action if somebody contravenes the order.

13. Get permission before renovating or altering your flat

Most leases state that permission should be obtained from the freeholder or managing agents before renovations or alterations are carried out to individual units. This is in addition to any permissions you must obtain from the local council.

The best thing is to write to the managing agents, or Residents' Committee if there are no outside managers, detailing the works you hope to be able to do. You should add that you are at the same time in the process of obtaining permission from Building Control at the council, if relevant.

Then, assuming there is no objection in theory, it is recommended that you circulate a letter to all residents, giving them details of the builder and building works, and stating how long you expect the works to continue. Reassure the residents that there will be no work after 4.30pm, or at weekends, and that you will make sure the site is left clear and clean every night.

All of the above will endear you to your fellow residents and mean they welcome you into the block. Every block of flats welcomes responsible, community-minded occupants.

WHAT IF PROBLEMS PERSIST?

Suppose you have an owner who does not pay service charges – in spite of many reminders. Or an occupant who continues to play loud music, leaves rubbish and rubble in common parts or undertakes renovations without getting relevant permissions.

What action should you take then?

Unpaid service charges

This is one of the commonest problems of all, and just about all blocks of flats will have at least one persistent non-payer in their midst. Most managing agents have a policy of dealing with this which is: they write two letters, then if there is no response, contact the mortgage provider. Otherwise, the next step is court procedure. This is another very good reason why it makes sense to have the block properly managed by outside agents. Interest is also added onto late payments, at, typically, five per cent over base.

Otherwise, if there are no managing agents, first of all try to discover why these charges are unpaid. Sometimes residents withhold charges as a 'protest'. Most often the reason is that they are short of money and can't pay. But it is human nature to bluster and protest and make out it is somebody else's fault.

Sometimes there is a genuine cashflow problem and very often, the best solution here is to work out a method of payment with the leaseholder which will be satisfactory to both parties.

If the charges are challenged, as they often are, and result in much paperwork flying back and forth, the judge may well order the case to be heard by a LVT, who will adjudicate on whether the charges are 'reasonable' and must be paid.

Then you will have to go back to court to get the charges actually paid, and the judge could order that they are paid in small instalments of, say, £5 a month, depending on the debtor's circumstances. You cannot get blood out of a stone, as debtors will often allege.

Persisting with non-payers can be a long, drawn-out process requiring much stamina and energy, but residents must not imagine they will be allowed to get away with unpaid charges. It is extremely difficult to win forfeiture of the lease, but in extreme cases, this is the last resort.

In most cases, the debtor will realise he or she is living above their means, and sell the flat. Any unpaid charges must be settled before completion of the deal, though.

More worrying is the situation whereby some residents refuse to pay an extra levy for building works, or maintain that they cannot afford to pay. This frequently adversely affects the building, as major works are only carried out when necessary.

No builder or contractor will agree to start the work unless they know they will be paid for it. Sometimes it can take up to a year to collect all the money due from levies, by which time the works may have to be re-quoted for, and costs will have risen.

If the non-payers persist, the best thing is to take advice from the non-profit making Leasehold Advisory Service, or to get a solicitor to serve an injunction. If the charges are disputed the case may have to be taken to the LVT anyway.

Persistent loud music

This is one of the very worst problems but, in a way, it is the easiest to address, as there are now laws preventing the playing of loud music to the annoyance of others.

The best approach here, after writing directly to the offender, is to contact the local council who will also write, warning the recipient that action can be taken. In any case, whatever the lease might say, you are not allowed by law to play loud music after 11pm.

The local council, which has a duty to prevent noise, will not reveal who has complained, but has powers to remove the musical equipment causing the noise.

Sometimes residents do not realise just how much noise carries in a block of flats, and will make sure the music is turned down, when this is politely requested. The thing is, nobody likes listening to other people's music and this must be respected in a block of flats.

Anybody who wants to hold an occasional party, where music may be played later than 11pm, should write to residents and offer to turn down the music if it is too loud. Another tactic is to invite all residents to the party who may be within hearing.

Flooring

Most leases state what kind of flooring is to be used in individual units. Some leases say that floors have to be carpeted – with the exception of bathrooms and kitchens – others that there must be adequate sound proofing.

The trouble is that although many leases state that flats should be carpeted, wooden floors are more desirable. You can now get thick sound-proofing when fitting wooden floors and this should always be done. Otherwise, to those living below, it sounds as though you are clomping across the ceiling in hobnail boots.

In Victorian days, noise was less of a problem because floors were carpeted, windows had thick velvet curtains, and surfaces were sound-absorbing. With contemporary design, everything is noisy – hard floors, granite worksurfaces and limestone floors are all noisy. Also, most people put blinds rather than curtains up at windows. All of these enable noise to richochet round the flat, even without loud music playing.

Before ever embarking on a redesign, check that your choice of flooring or worksurfaces does not make the place noisier than before.

Pets

Most, if not all, modern leases state categorically that pets and animals are not allowed. According to the Federation of Private Residents' Associations, this is the clause that is most often ignored. But pets are banned for very good reasons: dogs may bark, and cause immense nuisance to other residents; cats can smell and it can be difficult to organise cat flaps, litter trays and so on in blocks of flats.

In my block, the lease stated that residents could have 'small domestic pets' only. This prompted one new owner to bring in a couple of Great Danes. Of course, as soon as this owner appeared to be getting away with it, other people brought in dogs – a couple of yappy Yorkshire Terriers, a Rottweiler and others of less certain pedigree. Another owner brought in a parakeet, which got stuck in the lift, occasioning not only huge panic, but enormous expense and inconvenience.

The problem is, pets are anti-social in blocks of flats. If a resident has brought in a pet in contravention of the lease, the managing agents must write, confirming that pets are emphatically not allowed and that the animal must be rehomed. This policy must be strictly adhered to. In fact, if anybody brings in a pet, all residents must be circulated with the information that pets are not allowed, and that the offender either has to sell their property or get rid of the pets.

Humans are very attached to their pets, but rehoming must be insisted on, otherwise the place will become overrun with animals. And your beloved pets are other people's nightmares.

Forfeiture of lease
This is often held out as a terrible threat, but in reality forfeiture is extremely difficult to do. You have to serve a Section 146 notice on the offender but because of abuses in the past, where landlords served these notices for non-payment of trivial sums, or to evict people for not paying ground rent when this had not been demanded, the law has been amended since February 2005. It now states that you can only serve a Section 146 notice if the leaseholder has admitted a breach, or this has been admitted at a

LVT hearing. Or, they have owed a sum exceeding £350 for more than three years.

Otherwise, you have to take them to court. Leases can be forfeited for a number of reasons, such as persistently unpaid service charges and wilful flouting of the terms of the lease (e.g. playing loud music and leaving rubble and rubbish in the common parts). Although it has become difficult to serve a forfeiture notice, it is not impossible, and can be reserved as the ultimate threat, bearing in mind that if the lease is forfeited, the leaseholder loses everything.

Some experts believe that forfeiture of the lease is medieval and unjust. They recommend that, instead of this extreme action, the offender should be forced to sell their property and be allowed to keep the proceeds after all debts and outstanding charges have been settled. This seems fairer than forfeiture, and could be a much more workable solution.

What could happen here, if such a law were brought in, is that the offender would receive a letter from a solicitor saying that because of persistent breaches of the lease – of which they will have been previously warned – the freeholder has no option but to force a sale, and will be putting the property up for sale after a market valuation.

This would have the effect of removing the offender, but leave them with enough money to buy somewhere else. It is a law that could easily be enforced, but so far, no such law exists.

CASE STUDIES

Margaret lived in a medium-sized Victorian block in Central London where the roof had been leaking for several years, adversely affecting both the common parts and individual flats. A firm of quantity surveyors drew up a specification and put the job out to tender. Average quotes came in at around £100,000, which would cost every owner around £3,000.

A firm of builders was appointed but were naturally reluctant to start work until all the money was in. A year later, less than half of the residents had paid up. In the meantime, the leaks were getting worse and the block was losing value.

As Chairman of the Residents' Committee, Margaret appealed to the non-payers to 'do the decent thing'. They argued they could not afford it, that the quote was wildly over-quoted and that they didn't live there anyway.

By the time the majority had paid up the original amount, two and a half years had gone by, and the quote had doubled, meaning that everybody had to pay much more on top of the original quote.

Another, similar story

Things most often go wrong when there are large bills to pay. Another block of 33 flats needed serious roof work. A firm of surveyors drew up a specification which was put out to tender. The work came in at an average price of £130,000 and an EGM was held after the quotations had been circulated.

At the EGM, the majority agreed for the works to go ahead, and to pay their share of the work. The sums payable came in at between £1,000 and £8,000, depending on the size of the flat. One of the contractors was duly appointed and bills were sent out to each owner.

After the meeting, however, several owners got into a huddle and held meetings of their own, of which the upshot was that they wanted to declare no confidence in the managing agents, the Chairperson and the contractor. Nor would they pay their share, they decided, claiming that the quotation was 'too high'. About half the owners did pay their share, but not enough money was collected for the work to start.

So far, this is an almost identical story to the one above, but it has a different ending. It was time for the AGM, and time to vote that the agents remained for another year. Several of the 'dissenters' stood up to ask awkward questions about the agents, and to demand breakdowns of expenditure for years gone by. The meeting turned very ugly and in the event, the voting went 11–9 in favour of retaining the agents. The agents felt this was too close, that their integrity was put in question and promptly resigned.

This left the block, which had collectively enfranchised more than 15 years earlier, with no managing agents, no company secretary and no accountants, at a crucial time when works were impending, several owners were selling their flats, and a couple of long-term debtors were being chased up through the legal route.

Many residents now began to panic, especially as the agents were no longer taking calls.

What to do next? In this instance, the five directors got together and sent out a detailed explanatory letter to every resident, adding that the agents might reconsider their decision if there was overwhelming support from residents. The letter also included much more expensive price quotations from other managing agents.

The communication included a tear-off slip and a stamped addressed envelope to be returned to the Chairperson.

The letter worked. Not only did the agents agree to stay on until the works were completed, but the majority of the 'dissenters' who had not paid the levy, now promised to find the money. The letter was calm and reasoned but also tough, pointing out that all the flats would soon lose value if the roof work was not carried out. It was, as had already been pointed out, not an option.

The moral here? Whenever something serious threatens the integrity, structure or management of the building, communicate instantly, outlining the problems and their possible solutions.

IN SOME CASES, MEDIATION MAY BE THE ANSWER

A case like Margaret's can now be taken to the Lease Mediation Service. In fact, all types of dispute that may arise between leaseholder and freeholder, with the managing agents, or between leaseholders in the same building can now be talked through with an experienced Lease mediator, with the aim of working out a solution satisfactory to both parties.

The mediators are qualified lawyers specialising in leasehold law who are also trained in mediation techniques.

This is how it works: first, both parties concerned must agree to go for mediation. Then the Lease mediator will meet individually with each party to identify the problem and discuss possible solutions.

Second, both parties will meet together with two Lease mediators, when each party will be asked to confirm a willingness to mediate and to agree ground rules.

Third, each party will be invited to present their views of the dispute uninterrupted by the other. Then the mediator will summarise the issues and try to agree some common ground. There has to be a willingness on both sides to reach agreement.

How long does mediation take?
Once the parties have met with the mediator, it usually takes about three hours.

What happens next?
Suppose agreement is reached on the disputed issues, the Lease mediator will draw up a formal agreement and produce papers for signature by each party. If agreement cannot be reached, the case must proceed to the LVT or court action.

What does it cost?

In 2006, there is an application fee of £100 payable by each party, and the actual session will be carried out at the Lease offices (see Resources, page 208).

Advantages of mediation

This is a new idea for settling disputes which commonly arise in blocks of flats. It is low cost and without the horrendous stress and expense of going to court, where the outcome is never certain. It prevents emotions from running too high, and enables each party to see the other's point of view. The presence of a trained, impartial observer helps to calm the situation down and, often, stop a potentially fraught dispute from escalating into a full-scale legal battle where, usually, there are no real winners.

LISTED BUILDINGS

Many blocks of flats have become listed buildings – and they are not all elderly, by any means. If you buy a flat in a listed building, you have bought yourself even more problems, because you cannot undertake internal alterations, let alone external ones, without listed building consent.

For this, you need architect's plans which have to be submitted to the local council, and the planning committee will then deliberate. Do not ever alter windows or the external appearance of the place without being granted listed building consent as you could be ordered to take the entire structure down.

CASE STUDY

Claude bought a beautifully renovated flat in a listed building. After a time, he was astonished to receive a letter from the listed building department of the local council, ordering him to replace the UPVC window at the back – which had been put in by the renovator – with a wooden sash, as the plastic window ruined the integrity of the building, according to the planners.

Claude argued that he had bought the property when the window was already in and contacted the seller, who did not want to know. An intense legal battle ensued, and the upshot was that the seller, not Claude, had to replace the window at his own expense.

The moral of the story is, with listed buildings, you never know when a council official may come snooping round. You could also be ordered to take down a satellite dish or other TV aerial, replace plasterwork or original mosaics. In my block, which is a listed building, it took two years to source some mosaics for the front step which were near enough to the original to satisfy the council, at a cost of £450 for one row of mosaics.

Listed buildings can be a nightmare, so be prepared if you fancy a flat inside a beautiful building with a preservation order slapped on it.

CASE STUDY – WHEN THINGS GO *VERY* WRONG

Nellie, 79, lives in a block of six flats near Kew Gardens, Surrey. Most of the owners in this block are elderly, and problems started when the leaseholders were informed that the freeholder had sold on to another company. One flat was owned by the freeholder and rented out.

Almost immediately, bills for service charges began to escalate, and included an amount of £4,000 for gardening, divided by five. Initially, the owners got together and wrote to the managing agents querying the bills and asking for evidence of the increased charges. There was no reply.

Bills kept coming, and for very exact amounts, such as £236.48 for 'interim charges' and £441.22 'on account'.

In the previous year, the residents had been billed £319 each for service charges. Now they were being billed sums such as £421 each, for 'expenditure over the past three years' with, again, no explanation of how these figures were arrived at. The new freeholder informed the managing agents that these were for 'arrears'.

By this time Gordon, Nellie's son-in-law, intervened, as Nellie was starting to panic and shake whenever she received a new demand for money. He said:

We have never been able to get any satisfaction from either the freeholder or the managing agents, who we suspect are part of the same company, and we now have no choice but to go to the LVT, and we have to pay £300 to do this.

By now, the managing agents had changed and the residents were being billed £1,000 each, with legal action threatened if they did not pay.

This threat was enough to make the leaseholders of the other four flats cave in and pay.

The problem is, none of the residents has the strength or energy to go for RTM or CE. There is no possibility that either of these can happen. Also, as all the lessees are in their late seventies, or older, they feel they have not enough time left to go to all this trouble.

Gordon has amassed a huge file of paperwork, and the case is taking up all his spare time. He has embarked on it, he says, out of 'principle' and because he feels strongly that elderly, vulnerable people should not be harassed in this way.

This case illustrates what can still happen with leasehold properties, even where laws and regulations are in place supposedly to protect just these people. In spite of his work on the problem, Gordon – a former television executive until he took early retirement – has found it impossible to untangle the layers of ownership and management.

What can he do? Nellie is too frightened to do anything.

These are the possible steps

* The managing agents proudly proclaim they are members of ARMA. Gordon should contact Head Office and ask for details of their grievance procedure. He has kept all documentation since 2003, when the freehold was sold on. This step would not cost anything.

* Gordon can contact Lease, the Leasehold Advisory Service, and ask for their advice. This step is also free.

* He can contact a solicitor specialising in leasehold issues. This step would be extremely expensive, and there is no guarantee of success.

* He can go straight to the LVT. This would cost, initially, around £300, and would involve a long, drawn-out fight.

All these steps, whether or not they involve a monetary cost, take up a great deal of time and effort. Although this case may be extreme, it illustrates how very unsatisfactory the leasehold situation still is. It also shows how wily freeholders or managing agents can bamboozle the poor leaseholder with frightening bills, threats of legal action and general obfuscation as to who actually owns the freehold.

Many blocks where this sort of thing has happened in the past have got together and enfranchised, thus putting an end to this kind of thing. But you still have to be prepared for an almighty fight.

9

Buying Abroad

Such is the popularity of buying second homes in other countries that in order to meet demand, new developments are going up at an amazing rate all over the world in popular locations, many of which are specifically designed for second-home owners.

And by far the greatest proportion of these new buildings are apartments, rather than houses or villas. In Marbella, for instance, intense activity has been focused on the apartment sector since 2004, as houses and villas have become too expensive for the average market, according to estate agents Knight Frank.

In America, too, the demand from investors for apartments is at an all-time high – and the most popular apartments are high ones, too, with mid- and high-rise flats being overwhelmingly the most sought after.

But, buying a flat or apartment in another country is emphatically not the same kind of transaction as buying in England and Wales. For one thing, in most other countries the idea of leasehold is unknown.

You may say this is because their country did not have the misfortune to be invaded by William the Conqueror in 1066, and have all land annexed by the new ruler.

Whatever the reason, most other countries have made a success of apartment living which the British should envy – and maybe copy.

When you buy an apartment in most countries, you buy it in perpetuity, and you become a co-owner of the building. The way you buy apartments in other countries is much like the new commonhold idea outlined in earlier chapters, in that you buy into a self-governing community.

But this does not mean you can do as you like once you own the apartment. Far from it. All apartment buildings in other countries, in common with those in England and Wales, are governed by their version of the lease or the community statement.

This is a long, legally-binding document which you have to sign and agree to on purchase, and which restricts you to certain kinds of behaviour and also to pay service charges as demanded.

So if you are interested in buying an apartment in another country, you first need to get hold of the lease, or equivalent, and read it carefully, or get a bilingual lawyer to read and interpret it for you, if you are not fluent in the language.

This is most important, as many apartment blocks have very strict rules governing conduct once you are inside. In fact, most blocks in other countries have even stricter rules than those pertaining in the UK, so you must be aware of this in advance.

For instance, in some buildings you are not allowed to choose your own curtains or blinds, but must put up exactly the type as defined in the lease, so that the entire building looks the same from the outside.

In the UK, we are still not quite sure how we want to treat apartment owners. Should they be regarded as houseowners and allowed free rein over their individuality, or have their every movement strictly controlled by the Residents' Committee?

In most other countries, there is no such dilemma: your behaviour is strictly controlled and policed by the Residents' Committee.

APARTMENTS IN AMERICA

The USA is probably the strictest country in the world as regards what you are allowed to do in an apartment building.

One major difference between the USA and the UK is that with the former, you will almost always have to appear before a selection panel made up of other residents who will ask you some tough questions before they decide whether you are a fit person to buy into the block.

Most of these questions will take the form of a searching interrogation about your finances, as the Residents' Committee do not want to admit new owners who cannot pay their way and thus put the rest of the building at risk.

They will want to know, not just whether you can afford to purchase the apartment, but whether you can renovate it to the required standard, if you are able to pay the present and future service charges, if you have enough income or reserves to pay your share of major works and whether you can afford to pay the local taxes.

You will also find that there are extremely strict rules on whether pets or children are allowed. It is unlikely that anybody would ever be allowed to ban children from a flat in the UK, but they have no such qualms in the USA.

In one block where I stayed in Miami, Florida, children were emphatically not allowed, under any circumstances, except for brief visits. And no pets of any kind were permitted, not even caged birds. There were also many rules about sunbathing, use of the pool, outside barbecues, car parking, taking drinks into the pool area (only plastic cups allowed) and hanging out washing – no way is that allowed!

RENTING OUT

Very many people hope to make money, or at least cover costs, by renting out their foreign apartments. Again, you must discover whether this is allowed. In America, some apartment buildings permit rentals of not less than one year; others do not permit any kind of renting, while others are designated rental only.

Certain areas of Florida, for instance, are 'zoned' for renting, whereas in other areas you are emphatically not allowed to rent out your property.

Some areas of France have tight restrictions on rentals, as well.

Even where rentals are freely allowed, you have to work out, practically, how long the holiday rental season lasts, how much realistically, you can expect to get for your apartment, bearing in mind there is likely to be a lot of competition. You should also find out how much local agencies charge for finding tenants, cleaning and preparing and advertising the property. Unless you are nearby and very hands-on, you will have to use an agency and this could eat up at least 50 per cent of your rental income.

There will also be income tax to pay on the rental income, either in the home country or the foreign country. You really need the services of a good lawyer specialising in buying abroad – and who is not at the same time selling properties – to advise you on all these aspects.

Penalties for infringing the rules

These can be severe, as you can be sure that the Residents' Committee watch everything very carefully, and they will not hesitate to take action for any breaches of the mutual agreement or Deed of Covenant. First, you will probably get a letter from the Chairperson, or President informing you that you are breaching the terms of your tenure; the next step will be legal action to remove you from the building.

Because there are no leases, there is obviously no such thing as forfeiture, but there is such a thing as an enforced sale for persistent breaches which could leave you very out of pocket.

PROPERTY CLUBS

Property clubs are springing up all over the place, whereby you, the potential buyer, are flown out to a new development in Spain, Cyprus or Florida, for instance, and offered an offplan property at a supposed discount, usually as an investor.

By far the great majority of these properties are apartment blocks, and they are often, although not always, at the low end of the market.

The deals always sound very seductive, but investigations are now going on into these property clubs, as very many investors have lost large sums of money they have paid upfront to the club organiser. Be aware that these clubs use extremely high-pressure selling techniques and they may be better at selling than you are at resisting. If you doubt your ability to say no, leave these clubs alone and do your own research.

Very many developers, estate agents and others are pushing foreign homes as good investments. But with investment, there is always risk, and you need to ask yourself before buying what your main purpose is in the purchase.

◆ Is it to have a home in the sun?
◆ Is it primarily for investment?
◆ Do you hope to make money?
◆ Or are you just interested in covering costs?

But most of all, how do the figures stack up? How much deposit do you have to put down, when will the development be ready, what are the stage payments, what are the service charges, what can you expect from rental income or from 'buying to flip' (I nearly wrote 'buying to flop' – Freudian slip there!).

Also you have to ask yourself whether you really want to buy into a very cheap development designed purely for holiday lets. Some of those apartments are very quickly built indeed, and will not last long, or rise significantly in value. Nor are they always 'winterised' which means they are not suitable for year-round occupation.

THE COSTS STACK UP

Before buying an apartment in another country, whether for investment or as a holiday home, do all the figures, including the nastiest ones, before ever making an offer. Bearing in mind that, as in the UK, the cost of an apartment does not begin and end with the purchase price.

As with a flat bought in the UK, the costs will always go up with foreign property, even if the initial purchase price seems low, compared to a UK flat. In fact, there will always be *more* costs with a foreign property, as you also have to factor in the costs of getting there. Cheap flights are not always available.

Here are just some of the costs to consider:

There will be the mortgage to service, unless you have bought the place outright; there will be service charges, as ever, plus local taxes to pay, the equivalent of council tax, and utilities. In some countries, such as France, council tax is set at a much higher level than in the UK. Local taxes are proportionately higher in many parts of America, as well.

The thing is, these costs still have to be paid when you are not there. Most apartment buildings in other countries, as with those in the UK, are run by management companies on behalf of the owners, and they take their cut. In some upmarket developments, management costs can be very high indeed. There could also be costs for valet parking, landscaping the garden and decoration of the exterior – all of which have to be paid for by you, even if you are only there for six weeks of the year.

There will also be building and contents insurance to pay. Buildings insurance is of course compulsory, and contents insurance is certainly recommended when you are not there yourself. If you are intending to rent out the apartment, indemnity insurance will also be payable.

Apart from statutory costs, there will also be your own maintenance programme. Many homes in the sun need far more yearly maintenance than in the UK. And in common with service charges in the UK, you could suddenly be landed with a bill for your share of a new swimming pool, new landscaping, new security measures or a new lift.

These are all possible costs you have to take into account when buying an apartment abroad. And the more suspiciously cheap the apartment is to buy, the higher these costs could be.

Outstanding debts
In the UK, you cannot buy an apartment on which there are outstanding debts, as these have to be paid before the purchase can be completed. In some countries, particularly those known as 'emerging markets', the professions of estate agent and conveyancing lawyer have not really got going, so you need to make very certain you are not inheriting any debts for which you then become responsible.

This has happened in the past in Spain, although Spain has now become a sophisticated market, with less likelihood of this problem.

TIMESHARE APARTMENTS

The best advice here is: don't! When you buy a timeshare in an apartment, say for one or two weeks a year, you will still have to pay your proportion of service and maintenance charges, and these can be extremely high.

And if a lease is considered a wasting asset, well a timeshare is even more so. Many owners have discovered that they cannot even give their timeshare weeks away, let alone sell them, and that they have bought into a wasting asset which they cannot offload, but on which they have to pay service charges for the length of time they have bought the timeshare.

Timeshare is still being advertised, in spite of bad press over the years and comes in many guises. It is still sold extremely hard. For instance, whenever you are offered free tickets in a foreign hotel to some seductive attraction such as Disneyworld, suspect a hard-sell timeshare and avoid the offer.

Whenever you are cold-called and hear a recorded voice to the effect that you have won a holiday, yet again this will be a timeshare sales pitch.

You will discover, if you waste time listening to the message, that you have to attend a 'presentation' to claim your holiday. Once at this 'presentation' you will be given the hardest possible sell to buy a share in a brand-new apartment. Before you have come to your senses, you have got your credit card out.

Never fall for it! Never forget that when you are buying abroad you are buying, at least to some extent, into a dream and that is when your usual hard-headed common sense may leave you.

INHERITANCE AND SIPPS

It is not possible to put your foreign property into a SIPP (Self-Invested Pension Plan) as this tax-efficient plan was capped in December 2005, four months before it was due to come into operation. Properties abroad (or at home, come to that) cannot now be 'sheltered' from tax, and as tax matters can be complicated with foreign policies, it is essential to take expert advice on this before buying.

The same with inheritance matters. Whenever buying abroad, it is essential to make a new will, as many countries have their own rules and regulations about inheritance matters, and it may be that if you have bought property in that country, you have to abide by their very different inheritance laws.

Again, you always have to ask yourself: is this purchase primarily an investment, or mainly to have a second home in a wonderful sunny location?

The answer could dramatically affect when and where you buy, but no property in the sun will fulfil every aspect of the dream.

This does not mean it is not a good idea to buy an apartment abroad. In many ways, it makes more sense than to buy a separate villa or house, especially if you are not always there yourself, as a lock-up-and-leave flat is more secure and less worry generally than a house abandoned for months on end. Mostly, nobody knows whether you are there or not in a flat, whereas an unoccupied house is easy to spot.

But you will always have to pay your share of the upkeep of the block – and that must be borne in mind when considering such a purchase.

(10)

Conclusions

As we have seen, it is no simple matter to buy a flat.

Although there are now many checks and balances in place to try to ensure that the leaseholder paying a lot of money for a lease and then annual service charges on top, is not cheated and ripped off at every turn, the fact is that lessees still often have a mightily expensive and long, drawn-out fight on their hands when they want to increase the value and security of tenure of their home.

Over the past few years, very many firms of lawyers and advisers specialising in untangling leasehold law, have sprung up, not to mention the government's LVT and Leasehold Advisory Service.

The Citizens Advice Bureau and local authority Homeowner Panels also exist to fight injustices in the leasehold system.

The fact that leaseholders can now legally extend their lease to 90 years, secure the RTM and also collectively enfranchise, means that things are much better for flat owners than before.

But they are by no means perfect. In very many cases, freeholders cannot be found. In my building, we have been trying to trace the freeholder of an adjoining block for several years, without success. It has cost thousands, and we are nowhere. In other cases, freeholders may be large corporate companies who own very many blocks of flats. Again, it can be very difficult to discover who actually owns the place. Obfuscation in this area runs rife.

In other situations there is a complicated layer of ownership, with a freeholder and a head leaseholder to tussle with, before the residents can get any satisfaction.

Then the landlord or freeholder may own many flats within the building, which makes Collective Enfranchisement extremely difficult.

With some leasehold properties, leases have become extremely short and the cost of extending them is way beyond the pocket of the owners. This is especially the case when the owners are elderly and have only a pension to live on. Make no mistake, tough freeholders do not feel sorry for frail octogenarians who have only ten or so years left on their lease – and had no idea when they bought that the value of their homes would eventually dwindle down to nothing.

The matter of selling lease extensions and freeholds is part of the tough commercial world of property investment, and has become lucrative for freeholders and lawyers alike. It is no accident that over 50 per cent of the world's richest people have got that way through property dealing.

The continuing anomaly of leasehold tenures has also allowed freeholders and managing agents to be intimidating and threatening – and there have been very many cases of frightened leaseholders caving into the bullying demands of their freeholder.

Flatowners are themselves often to blame for their own predicament, it has to be said. Very many highly intelligent people who live in flats have no idea of the length of their lease, no idea who the managing agents are, and no idea whether or not they own a share of the freehold. Most have never heard of RTM, CE or lease extensions.

It all sounds boring and convuluted, so they don't bother to find out where they stand. Yet most lessees have paid well into six figures for a lease, the terms of which are quite unknown to them.

When I asked one friend, a journalist colleague, about the tenure of her flat, she admitted she had no idea. A few days later, she came back to me with the information that she had found out it was leasehold – and she has not only been living in the block for 11 years, but paying £600 a quarter to an unknown management company all that time.

'Do you own a share of the freehold?' I asked her. She looked mystified. 'Well, there is a management company...' she said vaguely. She is not alone, by any means.

I hope that this book will go some way towards explaining just how complicated flat ownership can be – even once the building has enfranchised.

So, is there any way of making the whole thing simpler, fairer and easier to understand?

These are my suggestions.

All new developments should as a matter of course be commonhold

At the moment it is far more profitable for developers to retain the freehold so that they can receive service charges and ground rents, and also sell on the freehold if they wish. Developers can also make a lot of money by selling the freehold to the leaseholders.

The government is dragging its heels over commonhold, maybe because it fears that if developers do not retain ultimate control over their buildings, they will not be so ready to construct new housing.

At the time of writing, commonhold remains a choice, and a choice which nobody has yet taken up. But if it were made compulsory, this would be a start at doing away completely with outdated leasehold tenure.

Of course, there must be stringent laws on the payment of service charges, occasional levies and any other charges which may be necessary from time to time to protect the building.

If all flatowners know for a fact that nobody is making a profit out of them, there would be more willingness to pay these charges.

At the moment, the requirement for service charges to be 'reasonable' means that a lot of time, money and effort is being taken up with LVT hearings.

It seems to me self-evident that the old lease system should disappear, and be replaced by a new type of tenure whereby flat dwellers own their unit in perpetuity, such as happens in most other countries.

What about non-payers?

My other suggestion is that the old idea of forfeiture should vanish completely, and be replaced by a system of enforced sale when service charges are not paid, or when flatowners exhibit other forms of anti-social behaviour.

What would happen here is that non-payers would initially receive a letter warning them that they will be forced to sell their flat if the charges are not met or if the bad behaviour continues. They will then be given a certain length of time to mend their ways and when this time is up, the Commonhold Association (or similar) puts their flat on the market, above their heads with no messing about. This clause would be firmly embedded in the Commonhold Community Statement, or similar, that all new owners sign on purchase.

Once the flat is sold, the former owner receives all the money due from the sale, minus the outstanding charges and costs of selling, redecorating or repairing. When the sale is completed, they are sent a breakdown of their charges. These cannot be challenged in a court of law.

There would be no deviation from this, and it would ensure (a) that anti-social people or those who cannot afford to live in the building do not ruin it for others and (b) that the former owner has some money to start again.

No requirement for reasonableness

If everybody owned their own unit in perpetuity, and the Residents' Committee was the only arbiter, there would be no requirement for 'reasonableness', as service charges and other costs would be decided democratically by all the flatowners.

As there would be no outside freeholder to pay, the only costs and charges would be those agreed by the majority of the owners. Detailed breakdowns of all expenditure would be sent to all owners annually, with the proviso that anybody can have a look at the original bills.

There would be a Board of Directors, as now, chosen from the flatowners and these Directors could be voted on and off the Board, as with any other directors. They would, of course, be voluntary.

There would be no opportunity for anybody to cook the books, or line their own pockets, as all sums paid in service charges would be for the common good.

Leasehold tenure would disappear

If Commonhold came in, eventually the old leasehold system, which no longer works, would disappear and along with it, all the anomalies we have discussed throughout this book.

When that day dawns, then flat dwelling would become simple, enjoyable and neighbourly, rather than fraught with disagreements, lawsuits and court cases, as now.

Resources

BOOKS

Callo, Kat, *Making Sense of Leasehold Property*, Lawpack, London, 2005

Cumming, John and Hickie, Richard, *A Flat-owner's Guide to Taking and Maintaining Control*, The College of Estate Management, London, 2005. To order Tel: 0118 986 1101. www.com.ac.uk

MAGAZINES AND JOURNALS

News on the Block (a magazine all about apartment dwelling). 1 Great Cumberland Street, London W1H 7AI. Tel: 08700 600 663. Email: enquiries@NewsOnTheBlock.com www.newsontheblock.com

ORGANISATIONS AND ASSOCIATIONS

ARMA, Association of Residential Management Agents, 178 Battersea Park Road, London SW11 4ND. Tel: (020) 7622 6126. Email: info@arma.org.uk www.arma.org.uk
The only professional body for managing agents. Holds conferences, seminars and training events for managing agents. A list of members can be downloaded from their website; also many of their publications can be downloaded.

ARLA, Association of Residential Letting Agents, www.arla.com
A list of accredited members can be downloaded from their website. All members are fidelity bonded and obey a Code of Practice.

LEASE, The Leasehold Advisory Service, 31 Worship Street, London EC2A 2DX. Tel: 0845 345 1993. Email: info@lease-advice.org www.lease-advice.org

The government's non-profit making service for the leasehold sector. Will advise on aspects of leases, disputes with freeholders and managing agents, and also offers a mediation service.

LVT, Leasehold Valuation Tribunal, 19 Alfred Place, London WC1E 7LR. Tel: 020 7446 7700.

A quasi-judicial body which pronounces on the 'reasonableness' of service charges, lease extensions, collective enfranchisement, Right to Manage and other matters concerning leasehold properties. LVT decisions can be appealed to the Lands Tribunal. Information from ODPM, see below.

ARHM, Association of Retirement Housing Managers, Southbank House, Black Prince Road, London SE1 7SJ. Tel: 020 7463 0660. Email: enquiries@arhm.com

RICS, Royal Institution of Chartered Surveyors. www.rics.org

FPRA, Federation of Private Residents' Associations Ltd., 59 Mile End Road, Colchester, Essex CO4 5BU. Tel: 0871 200 616. Email: info@fpra.org.uk www.fpra.org.uk

A non-profit making association which will advise on all aspects of forming Residents' Associations. Offers an advisory service to members, publishes a regular newsletter and a number of useful publications.

ODPM, Office of the Deputy Prime Minister. www.odpm.gov.uk

Publishes many leaflets and booklets about the leasehold sector, and Home Information Packs. Some are free, but there is a charge for the bigger publications. Downloadable information about applying to an LVT.

Publication: *Residential long leaseholders: a guide to your rights.* A PDF document; some pages are printable.

Department for Constitutional Affairs, www.dca.gov.uk

Information on commonhold

Housing Corporation, www.housingcorp.gov.uk
Information on shared ownership
Live/work units. Information from: Hurford Salvi Carr.
www.hurford-salvi-carr.co.uk

ORGANISATIONS SPECIALISING IN LEASEHOLD MATTERS

Rosetta Consulting Ltd., 31 St Petersburgh Place, London W2 4LA.
Tel: 020 7853 2282. Email: info@rosettaconsulting.com
www.enfranchise.com   www.rosettaconsulting.com
Will project-manage every aspect of CE or RTM, for a flat fee.
Enfranchisement and Leasehold Solutions Ltd. Tel: 0870 1123 357.
Email: anls@els-els.com
Leasehold Solutions. www.leaseholdsolutions.com
Brighton, Hove and District Leaseholders' Association, Cornerstone
Community Centre, Church Road, Hove BN3 2FL. Tel: 01273
705432. www.leaseadvice.org
(A non-profit making company which advises on CE and other
leasehold issues.) A DVD or video (*Escaping the Leasehold
Trap*) is available for £10 from: Shula Rich, 52–53 Kingsway
Court, Hove BN31 21Q.

SOLICITORS SPECIALISING IN CE

Dean Wilson Laing, 99 Church Street, Brighton BN1 1UJ. Tel:
01273 327241. www.dwl.uk.com
Alan Edwards & Co, Campden Hill House, 192–196 Campden Hill
Road, London W8 7TH. Tel: 020 7221 7644.
www.aedwardssolicitors.co.uk
Roiter Zucker, Regent House, 5–7 Broadhurst Gardens, London
NW6 3RZ. Tel: 020 7328 9111. www.roiterzucker.com

BUYING APARTMENTS ABROAD

FOPDAC, The Federation of Overseas Property Developer's Agents

and Consultants. Tel: 0870 350 1223.
Email: enquiries@fopdac.com www.fopdac.com

(Make sure when buying an apartment abroad you use a member
company.)

Index